TRANSTRATERRESTRIAL

Transtraterrestrial: Dark Matter and Black Divinities

Sage Ni'Ja Whitson

Wesleyan University Press
Middletown, Connecticut

Wesleyan University Press
Middletown CT 06459
www.weslpress.org

Cover Designed by Sage Ni'Ja Whitson and Devin Drake
Art Direction by Sage Ni'Ja Whitson
Layout Design by Devin Drake
Production Assistance by Julie Allred, BW&A Books, Inc.
Manufactured in the United States of America by Versa Press

Library of Congress Cataloging-in-Publication Data
available at https://catalog.loc.gov/
paper ISBN 978-0-8195-0199-8
ebook ISBN 978-0-8195-0200-1
5 4 3 2 1

Contents

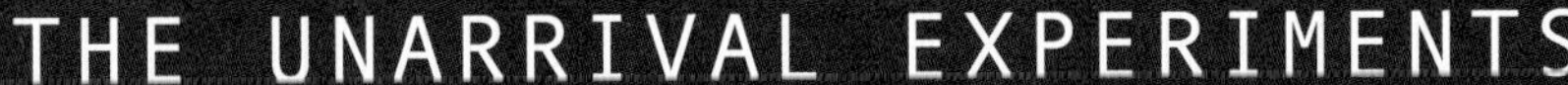
THE UNARRIVAL EXPERIMENTS

To the Reader,

I began this trying to find ways to talk about my work in a sacred scientific which superficially could seem mutually exclusive, but I have never felt that they were. And I believe what I feel. I believe what my body and belly, my marrow and gut bones communicate to me. And I know that knowing is old, ancient, ancestral wisdoms placed at my feet and in my hands telling me truths. Telling me nonsense. Telling me courage. Telling me tales. Telling me time. So as talking about the Divine emerges as a sacred scientific, I speak from a knowing that is nonwestern, divine, quantum, Black, Indigenous African, not yet, becoming, and refusing to become.

That said.

My mother
Aunts
Uncles
Grandparents
Greats
Great Greats

My 29-year-old *abiku*
child

Ọbàtálá

Elder Malidoma Somé
Elder Blackberri

Asé

2-4-6-8

This will be an experiment.
This will be a melody.
This will be a ceremony.
This will be an opening.

A RITUAL FOR THE FLYING

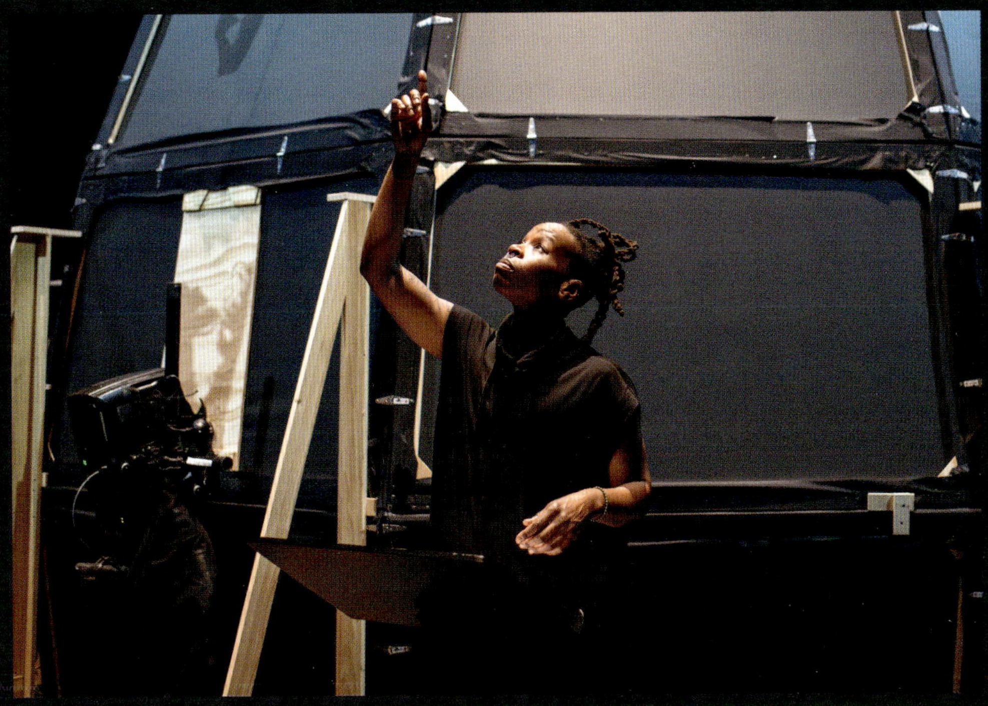

The body reaches itself in spirals through gender. It transposes galactic light. It carves vertiginous densities. Every time a splendid arrival, turns afoul vile expectations of ordinariness. Each fractal reflection inhabits the preciousness of a breathing ghost, with swells of purple particle lassos dusting what once held the quiet of a start. We've inherited and shepherd these rotations. To access the yes in our Queer skins is to invoke a portal to ancestral intelligences.

To un gender is to conduct the magic of living.
We fly, real winged journeys. And we must.

We are already ourselves
becoming.

Or refusing to be.
Whole,
in our
un

arrival.

We'll live adrift in the cosmic trails by which our bodies are threaded. Maybe
our lives will pass each other in the ether. Maybe
they will forgive each other for every time they forgot that they could
see stars up close, witness each other in past/future of them/we/selves.
Even if on the tongue
of a sharply evaporating second.
/ Maybe.

On the underside of our brownness is a meandering chameleon.
It creeps with black, a tiny solar system descends its spine.
Beneath
it licks at we.
Shifts
hue in slithering consonants
marks into we
and we change with it.
We slip
through selves together,
dividing supernovae.

Make we a crescent moon.
I'd like to see the possibility our dark made.

INTRODUCING THE CONSTELLATION

My Great Grandmother Willie refused to perform a body for me. or gender. Spell caster. Root worker. Black Indian. Medicine worker. Master Unarrival artist. Her genderlessness as an ancestor poured The Unarrival Experiments into me. Her refusal of (ancestral) materiality exemplified possibilities of an embodiedness or repudiation thereof. I use she/her pronouns here in the most other/all/beyond expressiveness they can hold. This ancestor is beyond. And she lived that way. She insisted a provocation of magical, cosmic, ancestral, Black invisibilities.

Not seeing her changed everything. It was one of her greatest gifts to me.

I don't know how my Great Grandmother identified. I do know as an ancestor she embodies an audacious agender possibility in fleshlessness. She reveals the technology of unarrival, the refusal to become.

Unarrival is cultivated by and lives in gender expansiveness and rejects historic narratives of Black liberation strategies. Unarrival undoes, disallows capture. Beyond simultaneity or multiplicity, those that unarrive are vaporous | bodies capable of filling a room with a mastery of perceived nothingness. It is a technology that does not end or begin at presence, and it will not land long enough to be made into a thing. Gone before becoming. Existing in the ante only long enough to change again.

I began The Unarrival Experiments research for a book project centered around my Great Grandmother and our potential Black Indian ancestors. Like many Black families descended from enslaved Africans, my North American Indigenous ancestry, at this time, is limited to oral history. My research began generally, starting with the Black Seminoles of Florida. *The Black Seminoles: History of a Freedom-Seeking People*, by Kenneth Porter, recounts the cruel, unrelenting hunting of self-liberated formerly enslaved Africans, a documented chase at eradication, where Black Seminoles pursued sovereignty from Florida to Texas to Mexico from settler colonialists, enslavers, and their accomplices (including Andrew Jackson's military who aimed to "return" escaped or otherwise illegally force-freed Black Seminoles into enslavement, aided, occasionally by some Native American tribes seeking potential favor or survival). In that text, I experienced impossible flashbacks, memories of cinematic overlays of rifles and pistols leading hunched shoulders in uniform in both the 19th and 21st centuries.

I'd see 2014. Where multiple police officers lined a Chicago street and put nearly as many bullets into the body of the 17-year-old Laquan McDonald as years he lived. 16 times shot. After he pulled up his pants, as he walked away from the danger surrounding him.

I'd see the Battles of the Withlacoochee, where the army advanced with rifles, burning and murdering everything in sight. Muskets and barrels, smoke and fire. Military and police uniforms, their firearms, and their dedication to genocide time-traveled me between forests, swamps, mountains, and city streets.

The hunted haunted me. And they were angry.

The Experiments, originally formed as complex live happenings based on my writing and amplified by dark spaces and technology, were the practices wherein i moved through the anger and the words and where i eventually received the medicines needed to move them out. But the conventional spectacle of performance: all the lights, all the white walls, the irises swimming in white sclera, were poised to absorb. To make milk of blood. The Unarrival Experiments became a constellation of art|works to put into practice for myself, by art and my life, a refusal. And i cannot take full credit. My Spirit guides made serious demands unlocked by my work over decades in centering them: listening, experimenting, rejecting, learning. I am living out Spiritual agreements made before i left my egbe for the first time.

HOW TO READ THIS BOOK

Each part opens with the ancestral veneration of my Great Grandmother (capitalized to honor her importance) and this "introduction." Hers won't be the only ancestral presence found in these pages. But hers will guide us through them.

What follows is a meditation, perhaps an unpacking of what is, at the time of this writing, a continuing, growing body of work. Maybe this will be a contribution to its living archive. What it will not do is be a stagnant reflection of a past. The work is not finished. These words shouldn't be either.

I offer you a provocation in book form that will not always move in horizontal lines from margin to margin. You will be led to move the book around in your hands, or your eyes, from here to there to follow thought and intentional visual movement on the page. I find that the conventional practice of footnotes and citations can insist itself upon an idea, where Black radical imagining is looking to be "proven" by some other thinker before it. I acknowledge that my work is in relationship to the worlds and ideas of others; thus, where those ideas present as tethered, as in water to seed, are direct quotes or originally published with citations, those can be found in the notes section. When a nonlinear context is required or an anecdotal intervention emerges, you will find a gesture of referencing that follows a writing-in-the-margins practice. This, like the book's structure overall, exposes the way my brain works and the way that this research has manifested. All flying, kaleidoscopic, multiple, expanded, simultaneous, images | words | as images | in pictures. The book structure asks you to stay in its time.

So, I have removed most citations, and footnotes, a bibliography, photo credits, titles, and the table of contents are in the center of the book at the end of – and between – the two books, *The Unarrival Experiments* and *Counterproposals*.

The Unarrival Experiments is a constellation of art | works, five distinct and overlapping projects, conceived between 2017 and 2020. In this section, I engage each project through a letter-writing practice i cultivated during the covid-19 pandemic shutdowns. From a four-letter word, i task myself (or others when in a facilitation role) to respond in letter form for four pages. Not all letters in the book will be four pages, however. The letter form has been a liberatory practice espousing love across times and water, advancing manifestos, declarations of rage, and suspense. I've come to welcome this as a rigorous writing practice in prayer. It feels fitting to speak back to a work from the embodied practices that have helped it come to be.

Counterproposals developed as my research became a universe unto itself, and the ideas yearned for ideas in words, not another application or creative transcription. A few of the texts are reimagined from performance lectures where I continued to experiment with the ideas out loud and made new sense of them for this book. They are a collection speaking to each other, which shares the theoretical underpinnings of my art projects.

Begin with whichever part you wish or whichever piece between them you are called to. Unarrive as a reader.

I. Book. Holy.

Dear, Great Grandmother Willie,

An obituary placed you, at some point in your life, in Paducah, Texas. I believe it was your son's, my grandfather Berry Red. Paducah then on to Kansas City, Kansas, is as Earthly as i know of you. At some point in time you were on this plane tending to plants and making medicines from the first healer. I imagine you moving the world around you, twisting the air as you walk. I see you, a soft, rough, able hand at the soil. Listening.
And it is a
fabrication.
I imagine
so that there is someone against the blades of grass, someone putting my hair in place, to tuck back my locs fallen across my face, those that yield to gravity as I bend to reach where you may have been.
Did i do it right?

Today i harvested garden sage from my land. I planted it over a year ago, 5 small plants that are now over 6 feet tall.

The bees have returned now that there are so many flowers. They reach.

A colony of bees together flies a collective distance of the moon to earth every day for their work.

You, Great Grandmother, become grey smoke.
Black hair. Then grey then black. You
in front of me without form, telling me to look up.

You
in a field of evening primrose, palms buried in moist
stems. You smell the fires to come.
there can be no songs after you
unless
they are choirs of eucalyptus and osha.

the nighttime in the forests of Washington state is alive
when the full moon lays its silver blanket there it becomes a sparkling planet
animals rest.
animals wail
distant tides cooperate in wild
i imagine you stretched in all the black sharing a wealthy silence
and in you i
create a formula for
nothing and nothing
pray to my past
bits upon bits
skin to remember
wait

shadow a dark while
nothing and nothing

break water
necks that make swans
                remember swimming

pray to my mouth
nothing and nothing
hands sweat pleasure
smell switchgrass
plucking long strands
to graze
closed eyelids

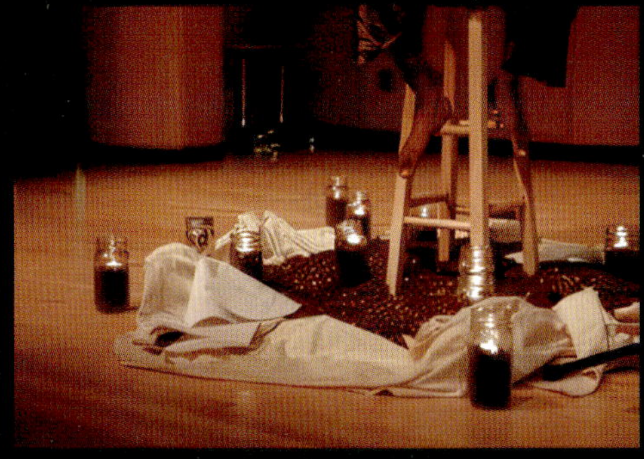

pasts in my east
nothing and nothing

before there was a name
noun
mud
or white eagle

nothing and nothing again

Great Grandmother,
                You are at the corners of each page of this
book
                and you spill everywhere.

Thank you.

To Our Futures,
Your Great Grandchild,
Sage

the night is a darkness in still gulps
cavernous inhale unfolding over hours
strange wonderous dances ask mythologies of the distance chittering
pulse making
a snap upon an infinite grid

at some moment in the moment of the night the stillness howls
untethered to bones or midnight it speaks in consonants
beyond a realm of human accord

greet you percussion first aghast
akin

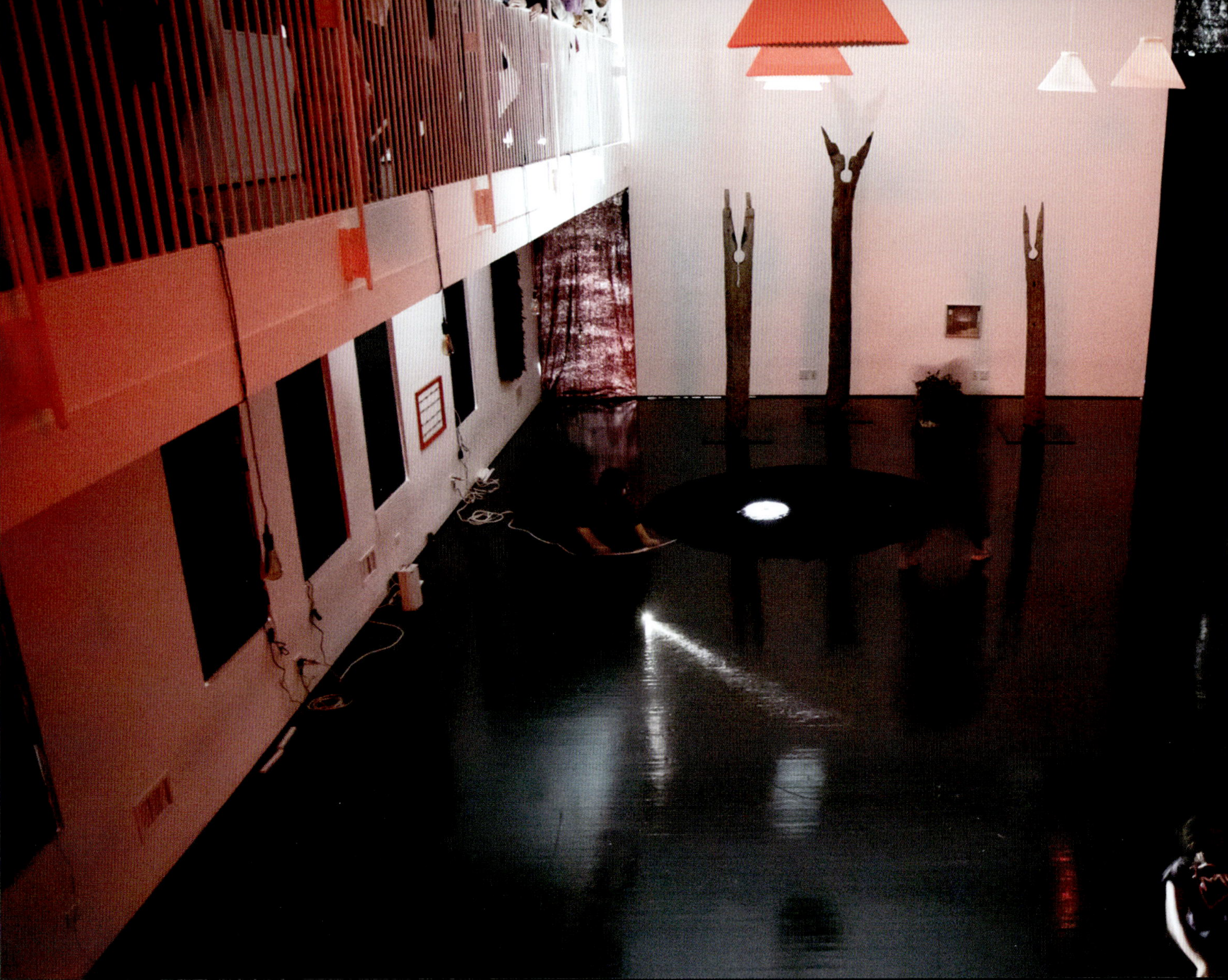

swallowing
mist borrows of
black
a journey down
tide wall of water
gasp fragmentation
an earlier grandmother

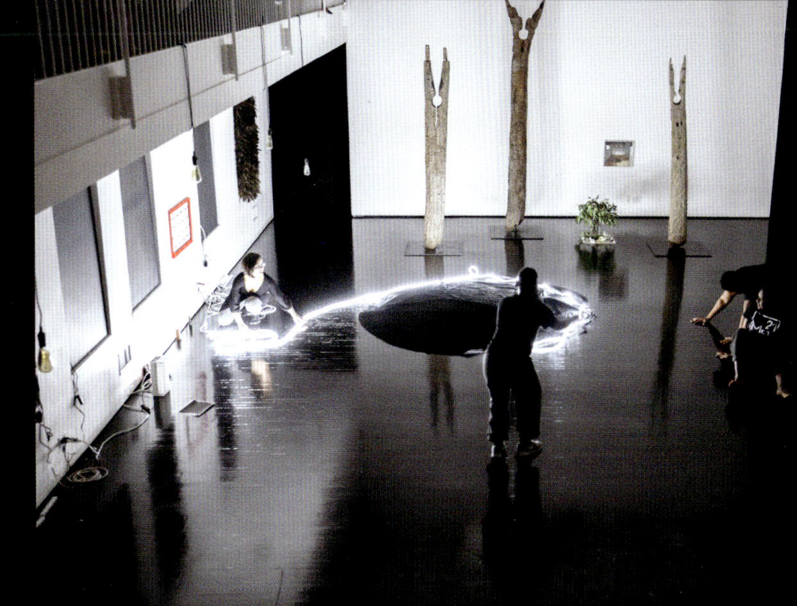

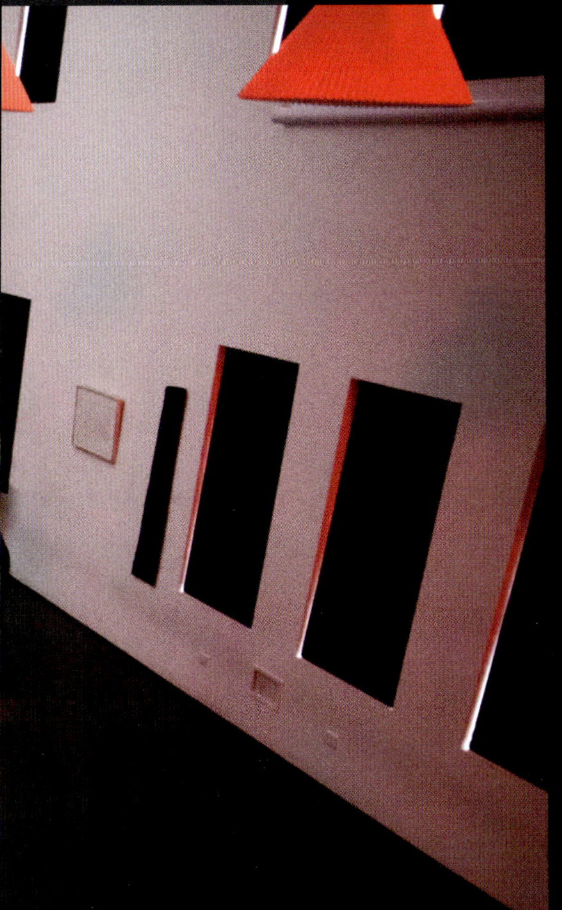

Do you have a fear of the dark?
What is your black sound?
What is dark or unknown about your body or gender?

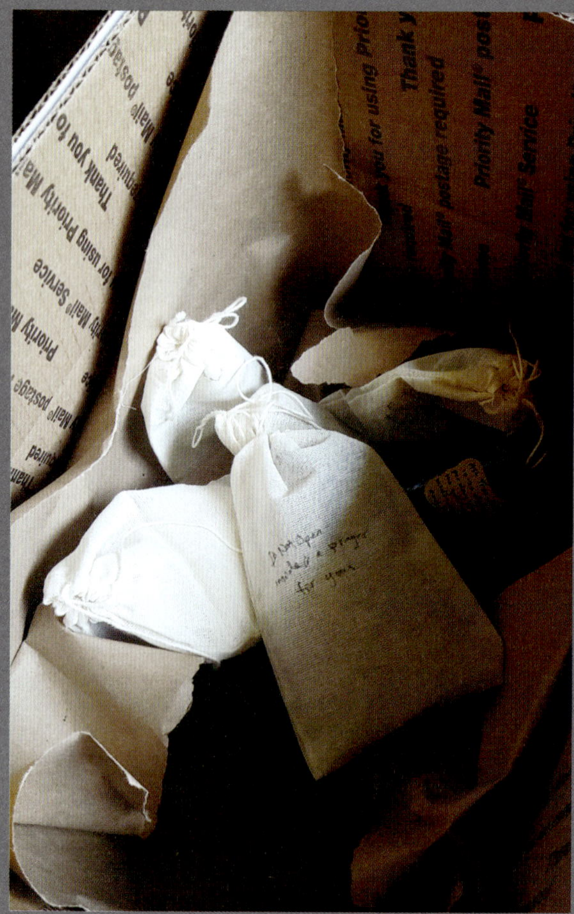

II. Dark Matter Cypher. Caul.

Dear, A Never Child,
you're in the bottom holding skeletons
the skeletons in your belly
bones between your teeth

I called my friend Jimmy and said, "Fam, i gotta talk to you about dark matter and dark energy." He said, "bet." Both of us, hip hop heads, science fiction fans, artsy weirdos, he, a visual artist and DJ, he felt like the right person to vibe out on unwieldly ideas. We shared ruminations on Sun Ra and Ancient Kemet, we laughed a lot, said "mmm hmmm," "right!," and "ok, okay, yes." A cypher over the phone, it was like two turntablists or breakers creating worlds on the 2 and 4. He said, "We have to do this again. We need to have another dark matter cypher," to which i exclaimed, "Yes! That is what we are doing." The name stuck.

salt water lifted
salt water drowned

In the first live cypher, i invited several artists to join me over three weeks for varying lengths of time. They sometimes overlapped, worked one-on-one, or, for those who were present long enough, worked with a few different formations of artists. Jimmy was among this first group. As per usual, i was deep in a development process with one piece and at the beginning with another. I call it a multych practice. We flowed in the cypher through ideas and projects and let ourselves make nonsense newsense out loud with each other. People were incredibly generous. It was a way of working that anchored the experimental praxis of the Unarrival constellation.

salt cast-offs
compose circle inscriptions

To cypher as a verb and to be a cypher, to be a contracting and expanding amorphous organism. Cypher because Black improvisatory music traditions have informed how my body acts, activates, and comes to know movement and ideas. It's the remix. The percussion. The play. The rigor at feeling a new something with all of you. The hearing and expressing at the ready with a group of people pulling from their depths. The black of it all. The trance of it all. The Spirit lift and breath and shake. Dark matter cyphering called us into the physical, atmospheric dark while exploring theoretical darkness, and conjuring metaphysical ones. It takes so much giving. It takes abandon of production/gig/grind logics. We, in the bottom, in circle, making noise as close to the salted drops as possible.

pull apart
pull together

The cyphers didn't always work easily. When folks were committed to being too prepared or overly directed, or when folks' fear of the unknown got in the way of them accessing their artistry, the cypher became performative. Cyphering also struggled when the balance of leadership and collective was off. I needed to be available, ready, and able as the conductor but in the room as a participant as well. In cyphering, i need to be as empty in practice
as i am full.
Nonetheless, every cypher formation made was the work. Every time. And what i also learned was that every time there are witnesses (as is true with any project), the introduction of a public changes the shit.

you're floating toward
riots unnameable
bear with the tearing
rips
consequence a start

The first and only cyber cypher happened in 2020, 3 months into the covid-19 global pandemic and national shutdowns. My studio became a refuge away from the wall of the apartment I as living in at the time, which medicined me against the encroaching madness made while project afte project was cancelled or postponed, when the only "job" seemingly unaffected by the moment was the one cops took on as essential workers murdering Black people.

I wanted Black folks to gather together. Be supported. Cared for. To try together. In the midst of new rages, i sought new possibilities in old practices. I made care packages for each participant after asking them individually what medicine they needed in that moment. I listened to them as they poured out their vulnerabilities and uncertainties about the world we found ourselves trying to survive in. Before we gathered again for the cyber cypher, each person received a unique herbal protocol, candles, crystals, a mojo bag, prayers. Care. Love. Something to touch.

It was beautiful.
And painful some.
It was exactly what it needed to be.

To Our Futures,
Sage

N S W

Rose. Prayer. White Carnations. Goat's Milk. Cowrie Shells. Melted Wax.

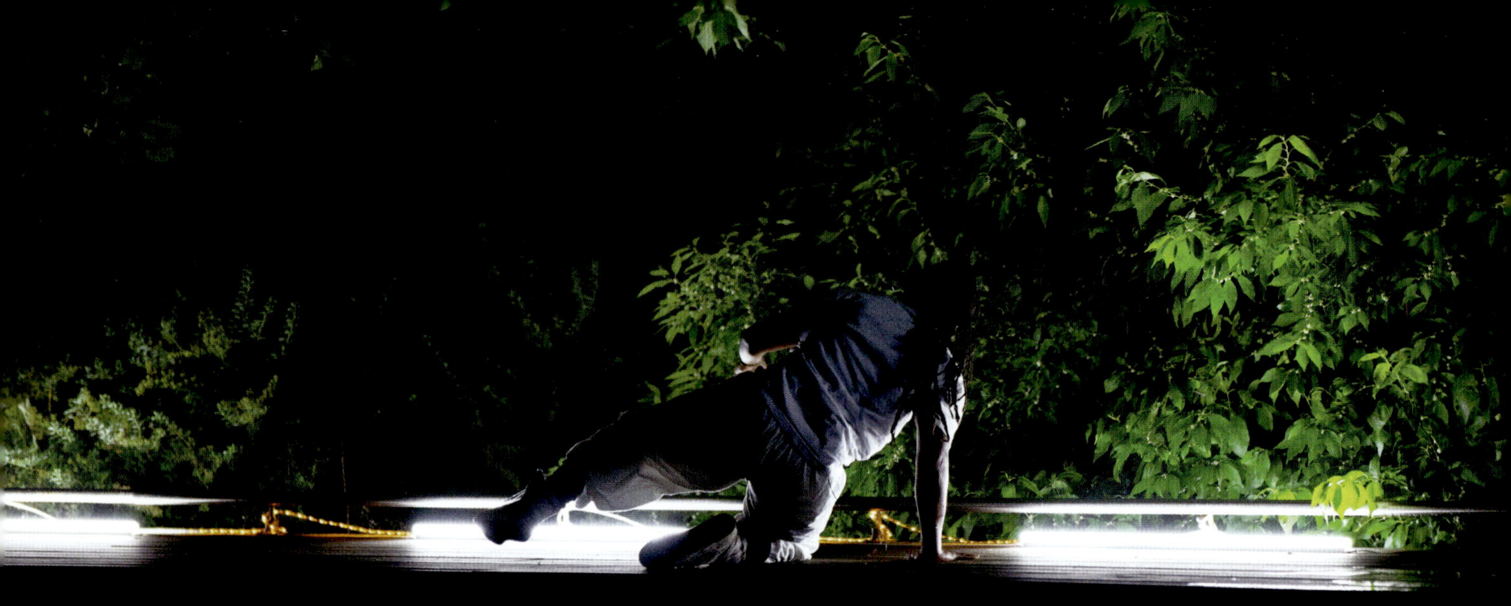

step outside over doors
onto the night
cold
groun
d
hear
abundant
nothing
revere
clock stars

two
lighted
candles
North
South
stand West
gaze
East

smell burning hair
darkened wind ——————————————————————

turn West
drop head
back   spill cranial seeds
                    simulacra
                    musical
                    notes shells
                    yellowdock
great
mother mouth
opens

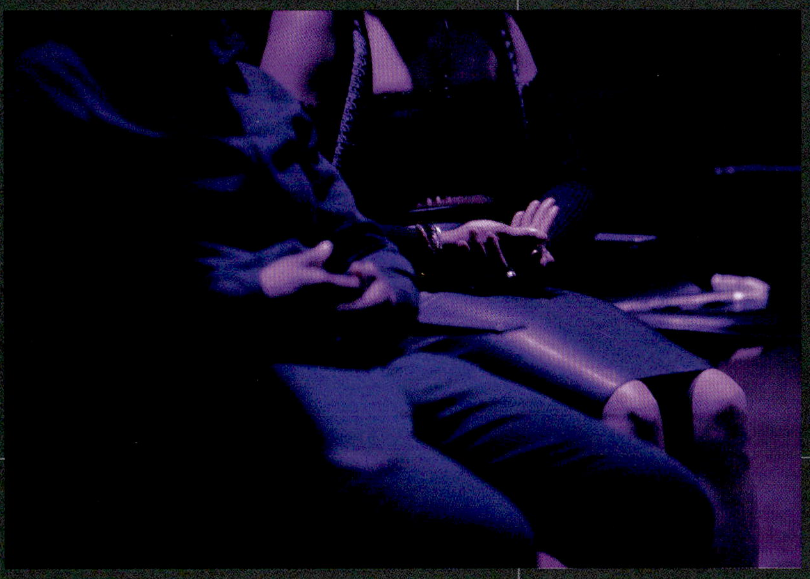

who loved you

the creases of seldom sun-kissed flesh impatient for the soil you wear
who hurried at you
to lay next to your bathwater

III. Transtraterrestrial. Egbe.

We will not lose ourselves when we return.
We will lose the earthly bits | trade them for
holy waters. We will drink | thirst after thirst.
We will be made plentiful at the site of our
first agreements. I only needed a way for us
to get to you.

After my ungendering surgery | i began
again.
Nothing fit anymore | i would be no longer
able to compress myself under names
or garments or people. The darkness
|while never a hiding place | had been an
environment where all the unwanted mass
or matters would dissipate. After surgery |
rebirthing | opening | the dark | the first
home and i recognized each other again.

Elder Malidoma Somé | nearly one year to
the date of his earthly transition | divined
to me | that i wasn't human. Not in the
theoretical sense | that isn't a diviner's logic
| he said i came here as a real kind of alien.

A something else | with important business
to accomplish with humans in this life. i
know that bringing people to the dark is a
part of that mission.

Through sweet meditation and reflections in
mirrors formed of smoked collapses | we fly
together to you in a soft expanse.
Black.

The hawk circles | They call at me from
time to time.

| *May i never land.* |

Egbe. Transtraterrestrial III.

i started with you in parts. Calling them iterations.
After several miles of words amounted to
language, but not a book, i began to see that
Great Grandmother Willie was again (re)directing.

i experimented in series after series making an
earnest effort of familiar processes repurposed for
this new work.
Breadcrumbs cast at my feet by my own hands.

Each offering concomitant failure and discovery.

i embraced it.

you were being called to trust that the
dark was enough

The experiments were an initiatory process where
i was being called to shed my usual. Listen again.

An epic experiment emerged at some point.
Raw, simple, and overwhelming for the audience.
Someone packed up their things and left in
the middle.

you were on to something
you were something

i needed to hear all of the words, all of the book i
thought had been written.

The incomparable Stacey Karen Robinson
swallowed each syllable and consonant of that
text like the sweet of an August plum.
Expert.
Exquisite.

or the dark.

i moved / chanted / choroused
Spoke aloud the poetry between expulsions of
sweat and fatigue.

It was much but not the right much

i had not yet fully invested in the principles,
techniques, or manifestations of invisibility

Transtraterrestrial III. Egbe.

in human form | i carried scars that when scratched |
bled black holes.

that was their first deed.

| *May i never land.* |

To Our Futures,

Sage

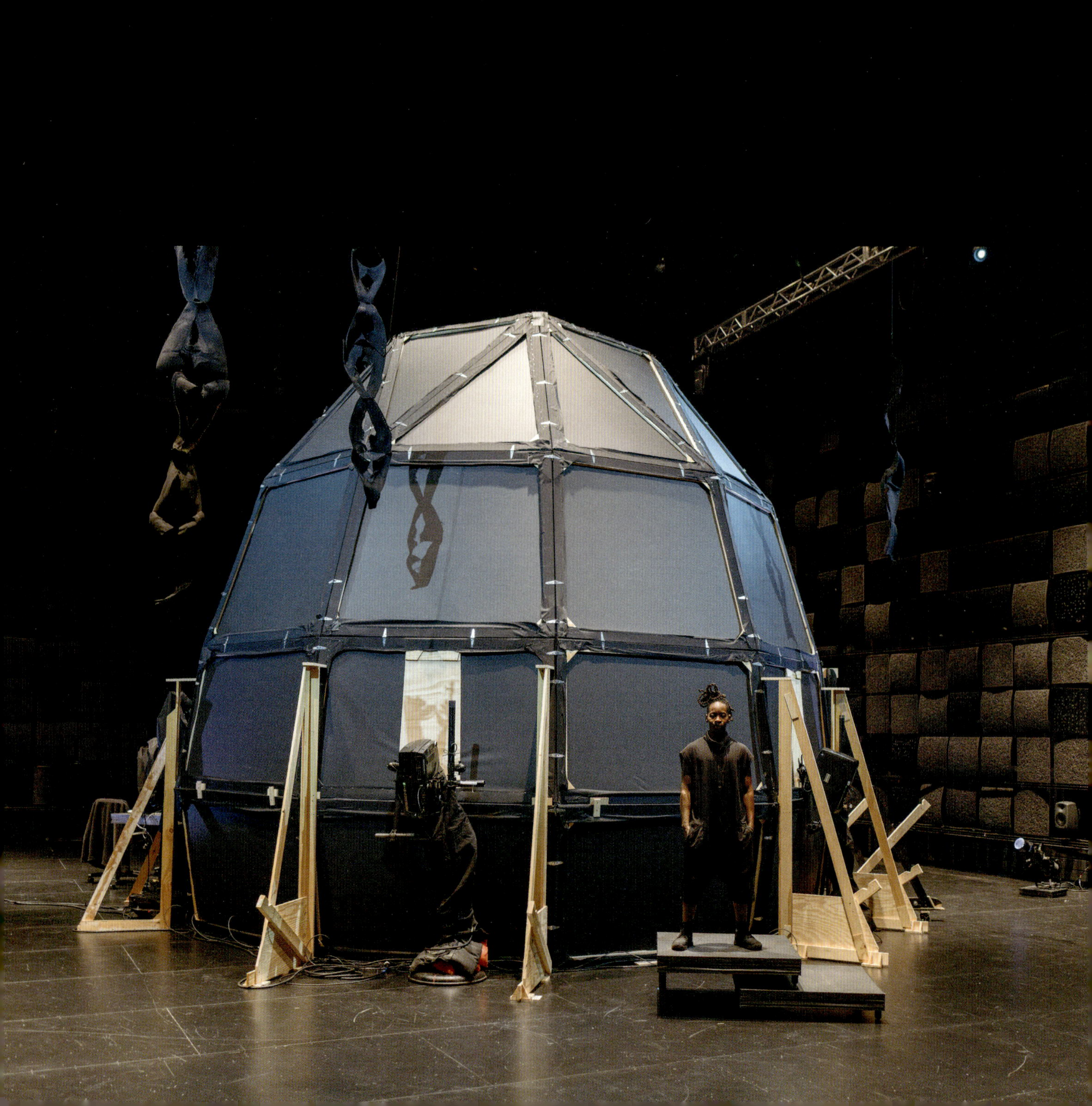

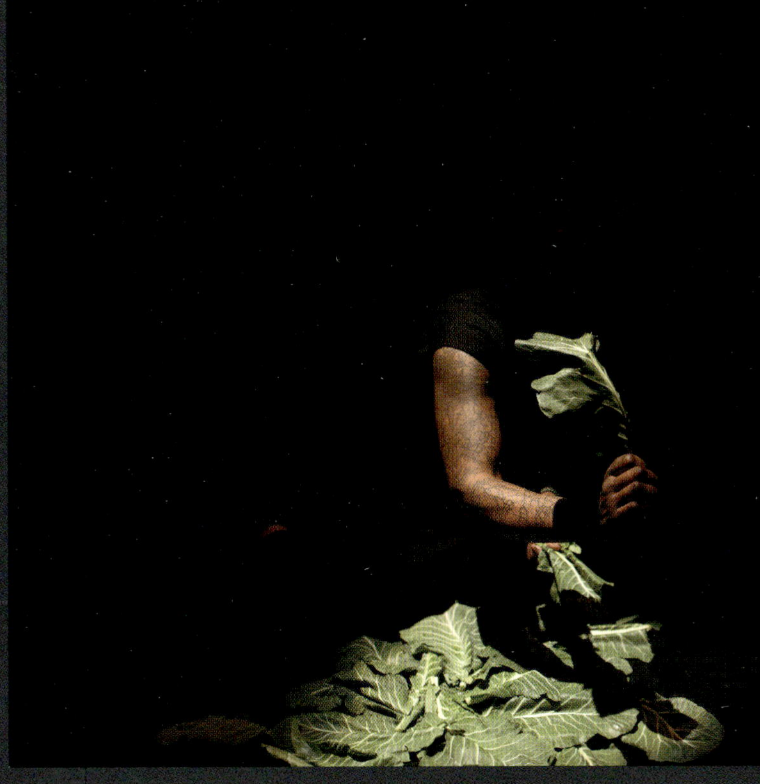

Shadows in the dark manifest multiples the way ghosts float themselves across a room
The sound of the body I can only see in dark trails
Make triads
Of me them us a song

Like weighted breath after a run
Or being under water – but when you know there will soon be air.
It is not a time for drowning.

IV. Illumination Catalogue. Lift.

Dear Great Grandmother, Willie,

In Hawaii i prayed, daily, at the ocean. The ancestral presences there are stilling. i went to Kihei to study darkness and astral presence at the summit of the Haleakalā volcano. Sacred land rigorously cared for by Native Hawaiians. My presence was not uncomplicated. i stayed in an Airbnb, contributing to gentrification and housing shortages. i traveled alone by plane, raising my carbon footprint. i paid a white business to "star-gaze" on the volcano at night. i tried to be a buoyant guest. i spent money locally, asked for permission from the land and ancestors before going to the water or mountains, and obeyed when they said "no." i made offerings. Sometimes, i did nothing.

While i worked on The Unarrival Experiments as a whole and tried to get a deeper spiritual and embodied understanding of the project's medicines, you told me that yours was not the only ancestral presence of the work to recognize. In fact, my entire practice of quiet being in Maui would craft the structure and methods of the Illumination Catalogue. i came to know that this was a kind of initiation into the work i was being called to do for transcestors.

Illumination was a play on words in the dark universe of The Unarrival Experiments – to illuminate or make visible, not to bring light or brighten. The space|ship and the egbe to which it was designed to fly are comprised of and exist as a site for Black trans technologies. My work for transcestors in rituals on lands across Turtle Island, alongside those within the space|ship, are ancient ceremonies. Each one instructs me on my human-oriented vulnerabilities and the wicked intentions of those who will not acknowledge that we are on purpose and necessary.

I'll never take the Pacific for granted again.

The Pacific in Southern California is often too cold for my body, which compels me to honor the water at a distance, brief with my feet as i conduct rituals and lay down fruit and flowers. All of that changed when i went there for an Illumination Catalogue ritual. Great Grandmother, i always feel you and my other benevolent ancestors; we are so transparently conversant during these periods. So, i know to do whatever you tell me to do, whenever you tell me to do it.

At the Pacific, prepared for ceremony, when i thought to leave, you said, "Do your work."

As i stood with one foot on the ground, exiting the car, a body was being pulled out of the water. I'll not forget the choreographies. Four people walk backwards, soften knees, stretch arms, grip shoulders to ears, then slightly bend elbows to hoist the water-dense body from the cold water. A white sheet catches wind and falls, covering death on the shore.

"Do your work."

My ceremony that day was for Camila María Concepción. She committed suicide, and the location was not made available to the public. Thus, i chose to honor her at the beach, where i could also close the LA work and release her from the week of ceremonies.

"Stay, Sage."

i walked down to my planned site, some distance from the white sheets and lifeguards, and went to work. i laid down roots and medicines. i prayed. i offered smoke. Song. Dance. Felt my legs heavy with a familiar grief. My body adorned in white, living, lifting, making air of the salted motionless to my right. Four years after leaving Maui, i found myself again at another ocean being told to take care of the dead and dying. i now embrace the Divine work of being someone safe enough to die with.

To Our Futures, And Our Dead,

Sage

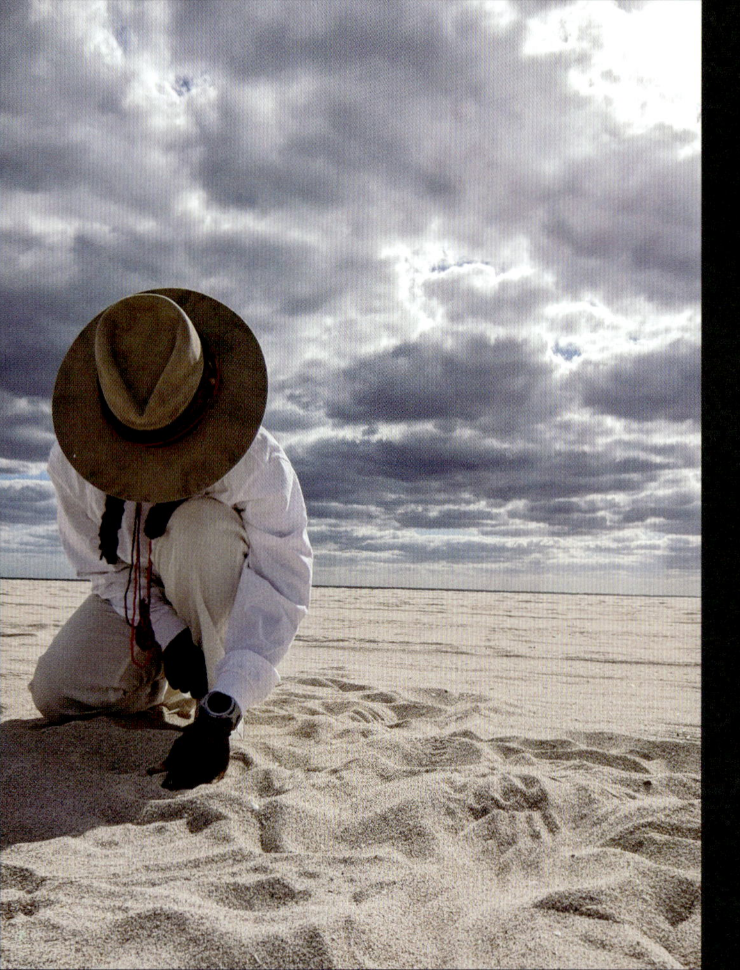

About a month
after my ceremony
at the LA Pacific,
i returned to the
Ocean in San
Diego.

i could again listen
to the water. i felt
my tender, my
work. Directions
remain clear.

The past always
echoes in the pasts
i visit as well as

become someone safe enough to die with
for a hatchling to stretch its neck as you create shade against its shell
ashen
a map stained in ocean floor brown it will never see

bring its mouth to taste its ancestors' home
make it a new one in the concave of a shell
cradled atop damp sand
let it die beside you
in the warmth of your hand

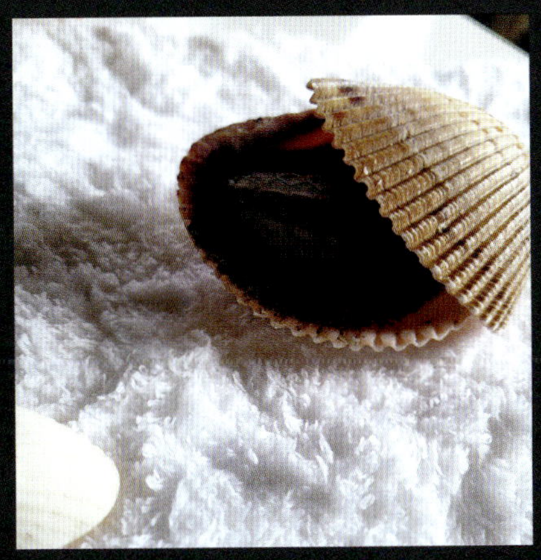

I awoke to an urgent desire to walk. My residency placed me steps from the Atlantic during mating season. The days brought red tides, tropical storms, and the witnessing of marine life and death. On this particular morning, i observed a turtle hatchling in the sand.
Because sea turtles come into the world at night, i knew this one had been beachside for hours in the morning sun, not likely to survive. Next to me was a complete seashell that i filled with damp sand and used to bring the turtle to the water. It moved with new energy, moved toward me, then stopped. i began to cry.
Animal rescue gave me directions over the phone: get the turtle out of the sun and away from the water where it is likely to drown. They will come to me as soon as they can.
i added more water to cool off the shell sand home and placed the turtle inside.
It never moved again.
The photo is the place i made for the turtle in my cabin. By my side. i prayed and sang.

HEAD
LIQUOR
RUM

Brown liquor. Rum. Red beans and rice. Scatter beans. Cover your head. Clean your feet.

BEANS
RICE
FEET

V. Space Travel. Wild.

Dear, A Future,

I will make this brief.
Keep going.

Even, particularly,
When the keeping is not understood Or is seen as wild.
That
Is not your business.

You belong up there.
You are of up there.
No missions to understand the cosmos without Black trans presences is complete.
We belong.
We are necessary.
We are galactic.

To Our Futures,
Sage

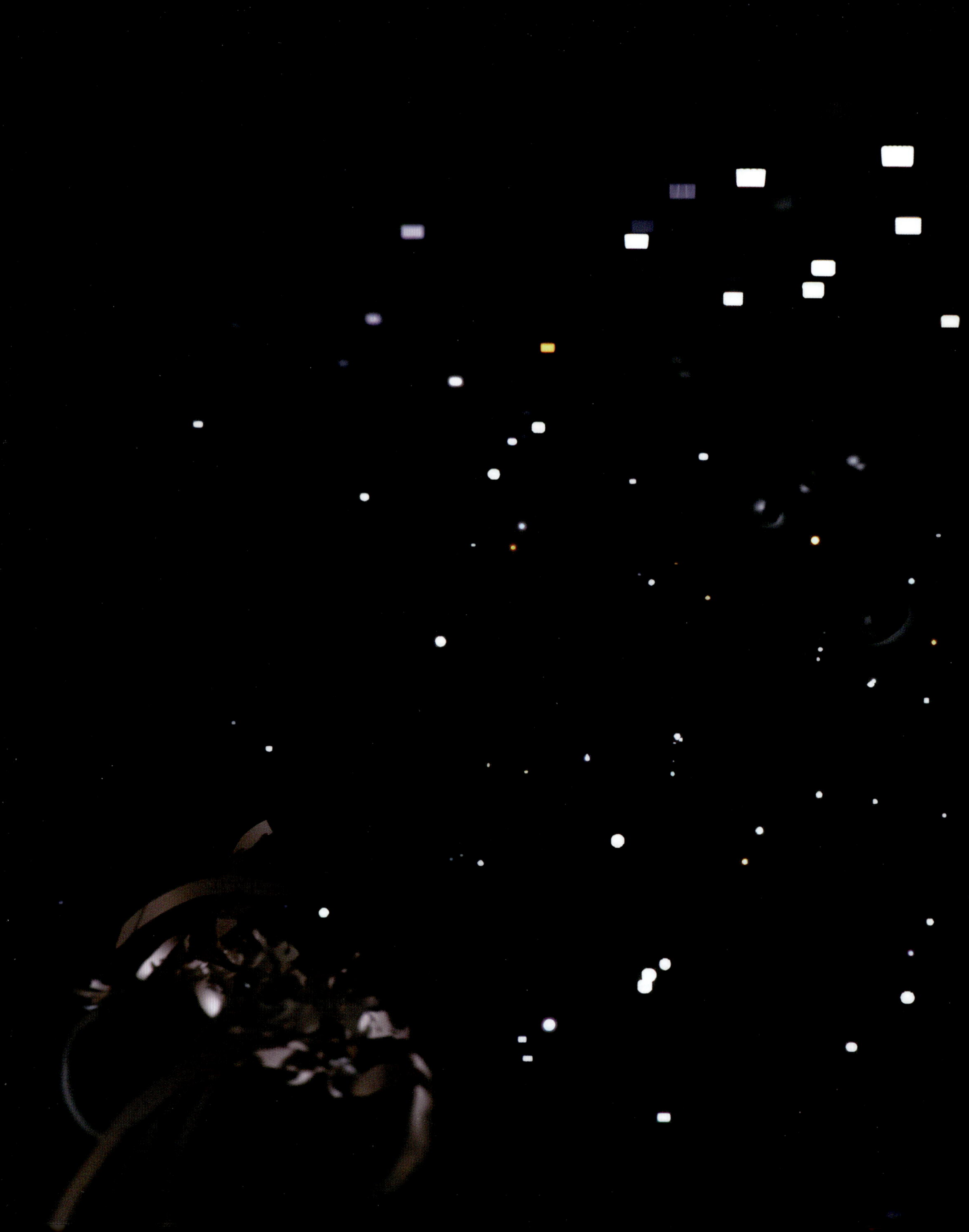

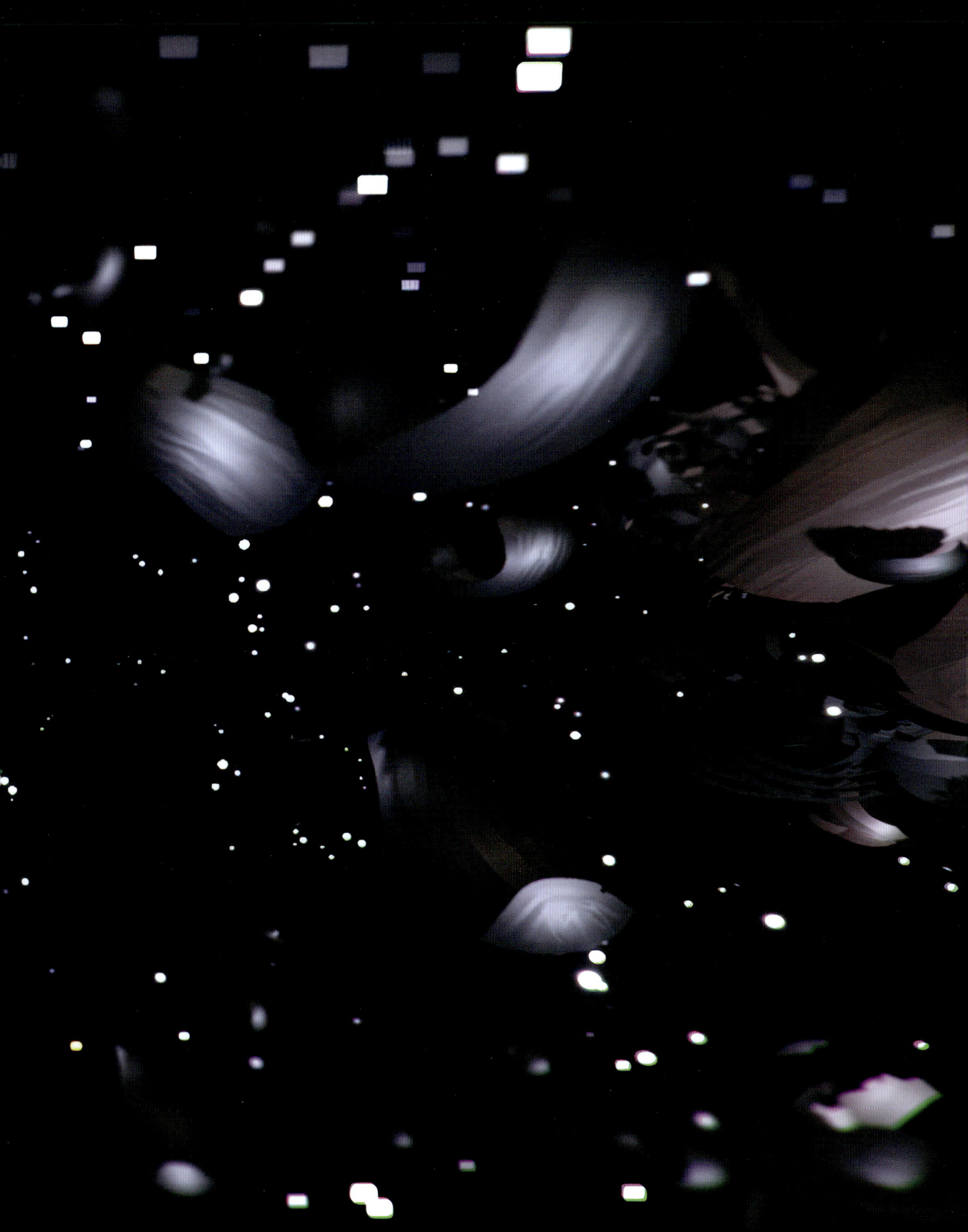

The Unarrival Experiments Image Archive

Transtraterrestrial, 2023 – Prequel and Premiere | pg. 9 |
Experimental Media and Performing Arts Center (EMPAC)
Photo Credit: Michael Valiquette, Courtesy of EMPAC

Time Trickle 'Cross You, 2017 | pg. 17 |
Prelude Festival
From approximately 2017 to 2020, while a significant volume of poetry and abstract writings were being developed under the names: *The Hunted*, *Time Trickle 'Cross You*, and eventually, *The Unarrival Experiments*, I engaged a series of performance experiments as a practice in corporeal writing that allowed for the development of more text and to understand its potential embodied articulations. This was an early theatrical, ritualized reading of a selection of material in the spirit "Theatrical Jazz." "The vaporous body" was an early shapeshifting practice and concept that draws from experiments in and with darkness, and the science of shifting states. This performance was a new exercise in the vaporous body practice.
Photo Credit: Courtesy of Prelude Festival

Dark Matter Cypher, 2019 | pg. 20 and pg. 21 |
Watermill Arts Center
This Dark Matter Cypher was the first improvisatory convening made available to a public audience. I was also developing Oba Qween Baba King Baba at this time (designed to be seen from above), thus experimented with a "dark dive" that positioned audiences in their own dark space one story above the performance below. The Cypher activated a concept of a "spectrum of darkness," where, rather than a proposal of darkness or "the dark" as a monolithic experiential, environment, tone, hue, or temperature, the spectrum moved us from the dichotomous phraseology of "going from light to dark," to proposals of shifting between different gradations, textures, or volumes of dark.
Featured: Kirsten Davis, AJ McClennon, Sage Ni'Ja Whitson, Tuçe Yasak
Photo Credit: Maria Baranova-Suzuki

Dark Matter Cypher – Cyber Cypher, 2020 | pg. 24 |
Photo detail of care/medicine package created for each Cypher participant.
Photo Credit: Artist

Dark Dive II – Weeksville Heritage Center, 2022 | pg. 26 and pg. 27 |
Site-specific outdoor installation performance inspired by the historic site. In order to be a gentle presence on the grounds and focus a *Dark Dive* outdoors so as to experience the darkness of a night sky, I created an installation of LED lights throughout the site. The first of the two photos is of the opening, where audiences were led through the grounds by way of movement and conjuring. Due to the rain, an additional space was made inside Weeksville for those who desired. The second photograph is taken during the Black Bath initiation.
Photo Credit: Maria Baranova-Suzuki

Transtraterrestrial, 2023 – Prequel and Premiere | pg. 32 and pg. 33 |
Experimental Media and Performing Arts Center (EMPAC)
Transtraterrestrial evolved from an initial series of performance experiments that began in 2018 through about 2020. In the beginning of *The Unarrival Experiments* embodied research, I worked with early text drafts from which to build site-specific installation performances. From there, I renamed a bourgeoning idea of a large-scale installation and sculpture as an "Unconcealment Ceremony." Eventually, the process determined that "Unconcealment Ceremony" described what was happening in/of the installation, sculpture, rather than its naming. It is also described as a "prequel and premiere" to honor that the EMPAC presentation was a complete gesture, yet an introduction.
The second image is of a practice I created called "collard drumming." Generated from years of working in percussion and rhythm-based erotic, Black, and African Diasporic dance (house, hip hop, West African, Órísá dance, BDSM percussion/impact play), collard drumming emerged to connect collard greens – a staple brought north by many during the great migration, and which tethered my tongue to my Ancestors' South – to a ritual of sacred instrumentation that ordered my feet as an improvisational mover for decades. The linkages between the erotic and sacred in percussion, my hands as healing instruments, and rhythm as vibratory messenger served to open each *Transtraterrestrial* flight.
Photo Credit: Michael Valiquette, Courtesy of EMPAC

Illumination Catalogue, 2024 – Miami, Florida | pg. 36 |

My body is a location as well as a visitor. These spaces cross roads of trap houses, projects, fields, hotels, parks, residential homes, alleyways. I return to these spaces to uplift their sacred lives and acknowledge the blood in the soil. In prayer, in shout, in solitude.

I do not always have the exact location where a Transcestor has passed, and sometimes, I assess or Spirit communicates that the locations are not safe spaces for me to conduct the work. In nearly all those cases, I hold the ceremonies at the water. After the many experiences I have had with death and life at the Ocean, I approach the water with even more reverence and attention toward the work they call me to do there.

Photo Credit: Artist

Hermitage Artist Fellowship, 2021 – | pg. 37 |

This image is of the sea turtle hatchling I was called to support through their transition.

Photo Credit: Artist

hull, 2023 –| pg. 40 and pg. 41 |

Transtraterrestrial is a journey led by space conductor, Trans Trappist the Extraterrestrial, a child of Great Great Grandfarther Black, the ancestor to time and the dark. Here, I invoke the Yorùbá concept of *egun*, our spiritual home before Earth. The VR material I created for *Transtraterrestrial* are creatures, vessels, and environments from this cosmic world, where Black transgender queers are the elders and secret keepers.

Photo Credit: Artist

BIBLIOGRAPHY

The following is the list of texts that have informed this work. As the book unfolded and the writing process evolved, it was clear that the citation conventions I traditionally follow for academic presses would not fit this work/world, so I released myself from them. What I offer you instead is a constellation of materials that I sat with, thought with, and argued with while writing this book, also to honor the folks informing "the room" of these ideas.

Abimbola, Wande. *Ifá Will Mend Our Broken World: Thoughts on Yorùbá Religion and Culture in Africa and the Diaspora*. Roxbury, MA: Aim Books, 1997.

Akomfrah, John. "The Last Angel of History." 1996. YouTube video, 45 minutes. Posted 2020.

Aleem, Juice, Kent Rigel, and Shantie Warriyah. *Afrofutures and Astro Black travel: A passport to melanated futures*. CreateSpace Independent Publishing Platform, 2016.

Alexander, Stephon. *The Jazz of Physics: The Secret Link Between Music and the Structure of the Universe*. New York: Basic Books, 2016.

Anderson, Reynoldo, and Charles E. Jones. "Introduction: The Rise of Astro-Blackness." In *Afrofuturism 2.0: The Rise of Astro Blackness*. Lanham, MD: Lexington Books, 2017.

Anderson, Reynoldo and Charles E. Jones. "Afrofuturism on Web 3.0: Vernacular Cartography and Augmented Space." In *Afrofuturism 2.0: The Rise of Astro Blackness*. Lanham, MD: Lexington Books, 2017.

Clegg, Brian. *Dark Matter and Dark Energy: The Hidden 95% of the Universe*. London: Icon Books, 2019.

Coney, John. "Space is the Place." 1974. YouTube video, 83 minutes. Posted 2021.

Fasola, Awo Fategbe Fatunmbi. *Holy Odu: A Collection of Verses from the 256 Odu with Commentary*. CreateSpace Independent Publishing Platform, 2015.

Glissant, Édouard. *Poetic Intention*. Translated by Nathaniël Callicoon. New York: Nightboat Books, 2010.

Glissant, Édouard. *Poetics of Relation*. Translated by Betsy Wing. Ann Arbor: University of Michigan Press, 1997.

Kreamer, Christine Mullen. *African Cosmos, Stellar Arts: African Cultural Astronomy from Antiquity to the Present*. Brooklyn, NY: Monacelli Press, 2012.

Marim, Natasha. *Black Imagination: Black Voices on Black Futures*. San Francisco: McSweeney's, 2020.

Morrison, Toni. *Playing in the Dark: Whiteness and the Literary Imagination*. New York: Vintage Books, 1993.

Moten, Fred. *Blackness and Blur*. Durham, NC: Duke University Press, 2017.

Moten, Fred. "Blackness and Nothingness (Mysticism in the Flesh)." In *South Atlantic Quarterly* 112, no. 4. 2013.

Okorafor, Nnedi. *Who Fears Death*. Chicago: DAW Books, 2020.

Panek, Richard. *The 4% Universe: Dark Matter, Dark Energy, and the Race to Discover the Rest of Reality*. Boston: Houghton Mifflin Harcourt, 2011.

Phillips, Rasheedah, ed. *Black Quantum Futurism: Theory and Practice, Vol. I.* Philadelphia: AfroFuturist Affair, 2015.

Prescod-Weinstein, Chanda. *The Disordered Cosmos: A Journey into Dark Matter, Spacetime, and Dreams Deferred*. New York: Bold Type Books, 2022.

Rubin, Vera C. *Bright Galaxies, Dark Matters*. New York: American Institute of Physics, 1997.

Shlain, Leonard. *Art and Physics: Parallel Vision in Space, Time, and Light.* New York: Quill/William Morrow, 2007.

"Holy Ghost," season 1, episode 3 of *Lovecraft Country*, created by Misha Green. Home Box Office, 2020.

"Strange Case," season 1, episode 5 of *Lovecraft Country*, created by Misha Green. Home Box Office, 2020.

"I Am," season 1, episode 7 of *Lovecraft Country*, created by Misha Green. Home Box Office, 2020.

TRANSTRATERRESTRIAL

Transtraterrestrial: Dark Matter and Black Divinities
Sage Ni'Ja Whitson

Wesleyan University Press
Middletown, Connecticut

Wesleyan University Press
Middletown CT 06459
www.weslpress.org

Cover Designed by Sage Ni'Ja Whitson and Devin Drake
Art Direction by Sage Ni'Ja Whitson
Layout Design by Devin Drake
Production Assistance by Julie Allred, BW&A Books, Inc.
Manufactured in the United States of America by Versa Press

Library of Congress Cataloging-in-Publication Data
available at https://catalog.loc.gov/
paper ISBN 978-0-8195-0199-8
ebook ISBN 978-0-8195-0200-1
5 4 3 2 1

Contents

Counterproposals

COUNTERPROPOSALS

To the Reader,

I began this trying to find ways to talk about my work in a sacred scientific which superficially could seem mutually exclusive, but I have never felt that they were. And I believe what I feel. I believe what my body and belly, my marrow and gut bones communicate to me. And I know that knowing is old, ancient, ancestral wisdoms placed at my feet and in my hands telling me truths. Telling me nonsense. Telling me courage. Telling me tales. Telling me time. So as talking about the Divine emerges as a sacred scientific, I speak from a knowing that is nonwestern, divine, quantum, Black, Indigenous African, not yet, becoming, and refusing to become.

That said.

My mother
Aunts
Uncles
Grandparents
Greats
Great Greats

My 29-year-old *abiku*
child

Ọbàtálá

Elder Malidoma Somé
Elder Blackberri

Asé

2-4-6-8

This will be an experiment.
This will be a melody.
This will be a ceremony.
This will be an opening.

A RITUAL FOR THE FLYING

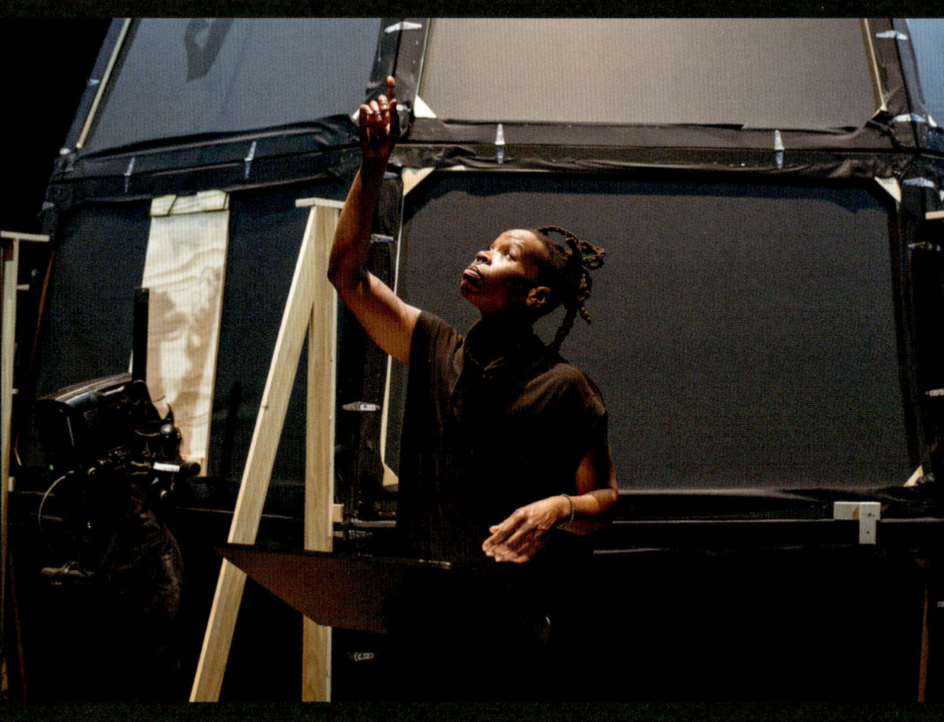

The body reaches itself in spirals through gender. It transposes galactic light. It carves vertiginous densities. Every time a splendid arrival, turns afoul vile expectations of ordinariness. Each fractal reflection inhabits the preciousness of a breathing ghost, with swells of purple particle lassos dusting what once held the quiet of a start. We've inherited and shepherd these rotations. To access the yes in our Queer skins is to invoke a portal to ancestral intelligences.

To un gender is to conduct the magic of living.
We fly, real winged journeys. And we must.

We are already ourselves
becoming.

Or refusing to be.
Whole,

We'll live adrift in the cosmic trails by which our bodies are threaded. Maybe
our lives will pass each other in the ether. Maybe
they will forgive each other for every time they forgot that they could
see stars up close, witness each other in past/future of them/we/selves.
Even if on the tongue
of a sharply evaporating second.
/ Maybe.

On the underside of our brownness is a meandering chameleon.
It creeps with black, a tiny solar system descends its spine.
Beneath
it licks at we.
Shifts
hue in slithering consonants
marks into we
and we change with it.
We slip
through selves together,
dividing supernovae.

Make we a crescent moon.
I'd like to see the possibility our dark made.

INTRODUCING THE CONSTELLATION

My Great Grandmother Willie refused to perform a body for me. or gender. Spell caster. Root worker. Black Indian. Medicine worker. Master Unarrival artist. Her genderlessness as an ancestor poured The Unarrival Experiments into me. Her refusal of (ancestral) materiality exemplified possibilities of an embodiedness or repudiation thereof. I use she/her pronouns here in the most other/all/beyond expressiveness they can hold. This ancestor is beyond. And she lived that way. She insisted a provocation of magical, cosmic, ancestral, Black invisibilities.

Not seeing her changed everything. It was one of her greatest gifts to me.

I don't know how my Great Grandmother identified. I do know as an ancestor she embodies an audacious agender possibility in fleshlessness. She reveals the technology of unarrival, the refusal to become.

Unarrival is cultivated by and lives in gender expansiveness and rejects historic narratives of Black liberation strategies. Unarrival undoes, disallows capture. Beyond simultaneity or multiplicity, those that unarrive are vaporous | bodies capable of filling a room with a mastery of perceived nothingness. It is a technology that does not end or begin at presence, and it will not land long enough to be made into a thing. Gone before becoming. Existing in the ante only long enough to change again.

I began The Unarrival Experiments research for a book project centered around my Great Grandmother and our potential Black Indian ancestors. Like many Black families descended from enslaved Africans, my North American Indigenous ancestry, at this time, is limited to oral history. My research began generally, starting with the Black Seminoles of Florida. *The Black Seminoles: History of a Freedom-Seeking People*, by Kenneth Porter, accounts the cruel, unrelenting hunting of self-liberated formerly enslaved Africans, a documented chase at eradication, where Black Seminoles pursued sovereignty from Florida to Texas to Mexico from settler colonialists, enslavers, and their accomplices (including Andrew Jackson's military who aimed to "return" escaped or otherwise illegally force-freed Black Seminoles into enslavement, aided, occasionally by some Native American tribes seeking potential favor or survival). In that text, I experienced impossible flashbacks, memories of cinematic overlays of rifles and pistols leading hunched shoulders in uniform in both the 19th and 21st centuries.

I'd see 2014. Where multiple police officers lined a Chicago street and put nearly as many bullets into the body of the 17-year-old Laquan McDonald as years he lived. 16 times shot. After he pulled up his pants, as he walked away from the danger surrounding him.

I'd see the Battles of the Withlacoochee, where the army advanced with rifles, burning and murdering everything in sight. Muskets and barrels, smoke and fire. Military and police uniforms, their firearms, and their dedication to genocide time-traveled me between forests, swamps, mountains, and city streets.

The hunted haunted me. And they were angry.

The Experiments, originally formed as complex live happenings based on my writing and amplified by dark spaces and technology, were the practices wherein i moved through the anger and the words and where i eventually received the medicines needed to move them out. But the conventional spectacle of performance: all the lights, all the white walls, the irises swimming in white sclera, were poised to absorb. To make milk of blood. The Unarrival Experiments became a constellation of art|works to put into practice for myself, by art and my life, a refusal. And i cannot take full credit. My Spirit guides made serious demands unlocked by my work over decades in centering them: listening, experimenting, rejecting, learning. I am living out Spiritual agreements made before i left my egbe for the first time.

HOW TO READ THIS BOOK

Each part opens with the ancestral veneration of my Great Grandmother (capitalized to honor her importance) and this "introduction." Hers won't be the only ancestral presence found in these pages. But hers will guide us through them.

What follows is a meditation, perhaps an unpacking of what is, at the time of this writing, a continuing, growing body of work. Maybe this will be a contribution to its living archive. What it will not do is be a stagnant reflection of a past. The work is not finished. These words shouldn't be either.

I offer you a provocation in book form that will not always move in horizontal lines from margin to margin. You will be led to move the book around in your hands, or your eyes, from here to there to follow thought and intentional visual movement on the page. I find that the conventional practice of footnotes and citations can insist itself upon an idea, where Black radical imagining is looking to be "proven" by some other thinker before it. I acknowledge that my work is in relationship to the worlds and ideas of others; thus, where those ideas present as tethered, as in water to seed, are direct quotes or originally published with citations, those can be found in the notes section. When a nonlinear context is required or an anecdotal intervention emerges, you will find a gesture of referencing that follows a writing-in-the-margins practice. This, like the book's structure overall, exposes the way my brain works and the way that this research has manifested. All flying, kaleidoscopic, multiple, expanded, simultaneous, images | words | as images | in pictures. The book structure asks you to stay in its time.

So, I have removed most citations, and footnotes, a bibliography, photo credits, titles, and the table of contents are in the center of the book at the end of – and between – the two books, *The Unarrival Experiments* and *Counterproposals*.

The Unarrival Experiments is a constellation of art | works, five distinct and overlapping projects, conceived between 2017 and 2020. In this section, I engage each project through a letter-writing practice i cultivated during the covid-19 pandemic shutdowns. From a four-letter word, i task myself (or others when in a facilitation role) to respond in letter form for four pages. Not all letters in the book will be four pages, however. The letter form has been a liberatory practice espousing love across times and water, advancing manifestos, declarations of rage, and suspense. I've come to welcome this as a rigorous writing practice in prayer. It feels fitting to speak back to a work from the embodied practices that have helped it come to be.

Counterproposals developed as my research became a universe unto itself, and the ideas yearned for ideas in words, not another application or creative transcription. A few of the texts are reimagined from performance lectures where I continued to experiment with the ideas out loud and made new sense of them for this book. They are a collection speaking to each other, which shares the theoretical underpinnings of my art projects.

Begin with whichever part you wish or whichever piece between them you are called to. Unarrive as a reader.

I spent the morning with manatees.

This 1,200 pound magical being has no enemies in nature.
They are not aggressive, do not attack, do not defend.
They do not need to.
Nature has developed a knowing of them to let them be –
Gentle.

A swimming relative of elephants. Whiskers instead of trunks.
All size and wrinkles.

They play.

They follow the water for heat. They remember.
Nature lets them be to remember.

Humans do not.

I want them to make it to a distance we can't recall. After human flashbacks or social media captures. I want them to be free from the concerns of our mechanized interferences
or snorkling crews who just *have* to pet and ride.

To continue to manifest an unbothered beingness.

And I dream that for my Black Trans self.

Manatee medicine offers that it is possible to be that big, that noticeable, that distinct, to take up that much space and to be understood by one's context as safe, kind.
For an ecosystem of care to be cultivated around you that holds your way of tenderness.
It is a longing.

The "blackest black" is a concept that has become a part of my working against the ways in which blackness and darkness are weaponized in distortion among disciplines that do not acknowledge the ways in which antiblackness pervades their practices. In science it shows up as a means to articulate what they do not know or cannot directly see, or even that which will die. In the visual arts, people like Stewart Semple and Anish Kapoor seek to create and own the "blackest black" manufacturing products that can be sold to the masses, in the case of Semple, or owned exclusively, in the case of Kapoor. In Christian dominations and in literature, the dark is often an ominous stand-in for evil or negativity. Darkness and Blackness in these contexts are antiblack articulations. Lazy. Colonialist.

Given this context, Transtraterrestrial begins with a Black Bath, an initiation into the dark. I am also introduced to the flight passengers (the audience witnesses) as the experience's conductor. This text ha been developed over multiple experiments across the world as ways to bring people into the work and, ultimately, into the offering of the space|ship flight. I share it here fully as an introduction to how to be with the work as it works on you between the pages.

Welcome.
Greetings.
We begin together.

In union under the sky In the Black.

I am your guide. They call me Trans Trappist the Extraterrestrial.
Half Alien. Half Amazing.
I am an old crescent and a future song.
Buried egg of a sea turtle and the Black hole's halo. I am the ancestor to dark matter and dark energy.
And I am their child.
A somehow time within time We. Together. Black.
I am here to teach you the medicine of darkness.

But first, you must be properly prepared. You must have your Black bath.
Receiving the darkness requires your
most tender. It may open you. It may unconceal you. It may ...

Body in the place where you are.

Notice, for this transitional moment, the darkness around you. Feel the dark in your hands, on your skin. Explore all of its dimensionality. Treat it softly. Like a beginning. Notice the way its edges meet the air and the darkness around you. Notice the fibers that create its corners and edges. Notice the dark. Notice what it is holding.
Now

Receive this, this dark as a portal. As a space | ship.
As a transportation device that allows you to journey the dark inside yourself and dark of the galaxies above you.

Now
breathe in. Out.
Once you have found your body more firmly against this space and this night, this moment and this breath …

Let yourself feel the dark inside you.
Let it glow and grow through you around you in your space on your skin.
Breathe.
Choose it everytime you need to remember you are here. And not alone.
Breathe.

See the dark in front of you.
Adjust yourself to ensure there is nothing but dark in front of your eyes. Aim for comfort and without any physical pain.
See the dark in front of you.
Blinking is ok, but keep your eyes on the dark wonder around you.

Now
Breathe.

Now.
Go back to the beginning.
To your first water.
Float in time with yourself.

Go back to the time you could breathe in fluid then again
Before.
Another spillage beyond the acres of seconds.
Go to the point of nothing.

See the walls of the space around you any fleshly anchors or conditions.
Let them become irrelevant.
Leave nothing but time or something like that.
Leave nothing but breath.
Leave nothing but the ancestor that is the dark.

Feel it around you.

I invite you to find the most comfortable position you can. You can lay on the ground here.
Or there.
Stretch out your body.

Breathe
Breathe
Breathe
Drink air into your lungs and let yourself be widened by it.

We begin again.

Dear, Great Great Grandfarther Black,

We ask you for entry, for permission to stunt alongside your glory, for we know that we hold magic beneath the curtains you've placed over our eyes. We ask you to open the folds of your dark draperies and receive this moment of us. Make us better. Make us hear. Here.
Great Great Grandfarther Black, we ask you to teach us. What does the dark want to say? What does the dark want us to know about this moment? What is it you have waiting for us beyond?

We ask humbly to be made here in the dark.

Say say in a spin
Dust us off in your indigo
Reach on into down through
Between the impossible corners call the skin of the cosmic bottom a manatee's back
Or an octopus's tentacles

Or that unnamed creature who lives in the dark black black dark
dark dark dark

You
Great Great Grandfarther help us to smell back blackness
Did you dream it here?
Direct the blood
To the pin drop of its source?

Great Great Grandfarther Black, how did you first know of a thing called illumination?

Darling I want you to listen …
I've waited for so long.
You're the only other half …

We begin again.

Newton Called it God

The cosmological architecture of Black / can be found in dark matter and dark energy. Dark / matter, the enigmatic force / so powerful it counteracts the pull / of gravity upon the universe / preventing it from collapsing / upon itself / Think about that / A moment in gravity / Inset prideful tales of apples and trees / White men / seeing and thinking / Insert / discovery / insert disbelief / insert repeated seeing and thinking / insert / additional disbelief / insert / eventual acceptance / Celebration / Insert steps closer to knowing / that thing / those things / dancing in assumed infinitum above our heads / called "the universe" / It must be said that gravity itself / although colloquially perceived / as one of the most powerful forces in the universe / is in actuality the weakest / as far as those forces go / And it is its failing negotiation / with dark / energy that makes the universe / (as we know it) / possible / Right now / scientists say we don't know / and can't know / the beginnings of the universe because the technology that would allow us / to see far enough into the past / does not yet exist / For now / 96 percent of the universe is Black / and unknown / Black and unknown / math is an architecture of being / Black / dense and unknown is not zero / It is 96 / Is dark / energy Black / magic acting upon the cosmos / Is dark / energy the constitutive element of Black magic / Dark matter is the aspect of the universe / that early astronomers could not explain / Newton called it God / Nothing: / a shepherd into the densities / of God / Zero is not nothing / It is the unseeable / unknown / uncontainable light / a Black so Black [dark] it's dark [Black] / "Inhomogeneities make / the universe possible" / Dark matter is the body / the stuff / Dark energy / the motion that precedes / thought / wherein matter exists / merely to make motion / actionable / thus, Blackness / is motion / Then matter / Time is the space / between / inactionable matter and motion /

It will not be contained.

Perhaps anti-Black violence in all the / inventive approaches / employed / in / attempts
/ at Black / death / and control / was /
really an attempt / to contain illumination. /
What we know / is / in their / absences / the universe / quite literally / would / implode.

Black is the color
True / Love

You. Here.
Check into your breath.
Take wind into your belly.
Mmm hmmm.
You don't have to decide to breathe,
decide to live.
Some of you can
decide.

Go back to the beginning.
When the night became something other than the dark holding you
or just the other side of day.
Go back to before frightful mysteries of shadows lived under your bed.
Can you recall a time before that fear?

Breathe.

Can you hold the hand of the child in you that understood darkness as a space of birthing?

Place one hand in the other. If you are left-handed, place your right hand in your left hand. If you are right-handed, let your right hand hold your left. The hand on top is that of your child self.
While cradling that hand in your other hand, turn it palm side up.

Keep your eyes open.

In the center of that open hand is a seed. Feel it there. Name it.
What do you need? What is this seed offering you to plant and nourish?
What do you need? What do you need to sit in the dark with your whole self?
To be that kind of free?
Imbue the seed with that longing. Go.

Enclose the seed in your hand and gather warmth around it.
Germinate it with the heat of your body and water from your perspiration, you are feeding it.
You are.
You.
Now from your seat, plant it in the dark.
In the air somewhere around you or at your feet or behind your ear or at your heart.

It requires the dark to become itself. So do you.
This rebirthing, this feeding, this technology of manifestation is in the dark … first.

Go back to the beginning.

Before the children of Great Great Grandfarther Black scared you.
When dark skin looked like blessing.
Before it was dangerous to wear melanin like a halo showering the body with dark cosmic dreams / possibility / Divine knowledge.
Go back to before you were taught it was less.
Than.
Or that light was the redemption in a day's
passing. And that white was the light.

Time is in front of you.
Here. See in the dark.
See the dark.

To the dark cosmic halo holders know that Great Great Grandfarther Black has gifted upon you a slice of galactic matter, energy, and beingness. You. Got this. In and of you.

the blackest black
The blackest black is underneath my mother's fingernails and is a pulpit
Hot in Ohio
The blackest black is my gender transition and the making of myself
The blackest black is a corner store in Detroit or bodega in Brooklyn
The blackest black is a sorrow in Georgia, red earthed piles of stones washed by the blood of lynched uncle or godmother
The blackest black is a cobalt miner in the Congo
The blackest black is the curiosity of a 14-year-old violinist with locs and chocolate fingertips
It is a collard greens garden\new years eve pig heads
Black eyed peas and prayer
It is kick ball with adopted cousins
The blackest black is

Tweelde deedle dee Skee ball
The blackest black is the dreamer in Compton tying shoes holding a purple popsicle in their mouth
It is a slip showing
It is a backbone slip
It is a back torn apart at the flesh
The blackest black is the neighbor who will tell your momma you cut school or pierced your nose or celebrates your high school graduation
The blackest black is Big Freedia's "You already knoooow," Abbey Lincoln's scream and the Wu-Tang Clan's "soooo!"
It is grits
and efun
moi moi
The blackest black is a transwoman in her 90s
It is invisibility and the power of the refusal to become
The blackest black is fucking up that dance and your algorithm

It's time.
We begin again.
We move to journey the dark together.

Breathe.

I'm here, but have come from far away. *Eu venho de longe.*
I'm going to put my palm into heat. Some liquid without wet.
Going to slice into a giant gaseous cosmic cluster.
Walk bridges that rise from swamps.
Say "fuck" three times. Now four times.
Glide us in something we can't retrieve without the back of the throat or stomach lining.
While in my first fulltime teaching position (at an institution who shall not here be named) I laid on my acupuncturist's table for the umpteenth time to treat back pain. I was experiencing debilitating spasms, daily, unrelenting. I was teaching between four and six classes a semester and was at the start of my transition away from using she/her pronouns. This time, at the head of the table, was my acupuncturist's partner, a magical energy worker and physical therapist who was called in to intervene in my treatment. She placed her hands under my head and said, "hmmm," "this isn't physical. What is it that you need to say that you are not saying?" After tears and consultations with wise ones (thank you to the Coalition of Diasporan Scholars Moving, to Onye Ozuzu, and Dear One, Omi Osun Joni L. Jones) I resigned from my position, committed to change my relationship to academia and to my art, reclaiming the latter as my priority. All of those healers, in their own ways taught me about the injuries of blood stasis.

I'll return to the blood

Healing on a quantum level
has already happened

Healing then
has already happened

Healing then
in the temporary temporal
is that of repair
The journey of repair on
this plane
toward that which has
actually
already occurred

Healing then
is *the* act
where the choices we make
in journeys of
disillusioned repair
derails the healing we are to
step into

You have to forgive me.
I have been dreaming in music.

Repair is implied in the words
"You have what you need"
"You can do this"
"Trouble don't last always"

But repair and healing aren't the same
healing isn't passive
isn't a witness in wait

It doesn't reach around a traveled track And
pull along a believer
weary from the beat up
and pulled down

I'm climbing over walls to write this
In the darkness of everything
Darkness meaning the seed and fruit
Black beginnings of life

Healing doesn't wait
It is a future, however
and there is no healed (a past tensed e-d)
There is a future where
the memory of the pain
gets absorbed in sound
The looping has multiplied to so many roads
that its selves are too many to be recognized only as
The One
Rotten
Thing
that started it all

There isn't a healed but there is a symphony

Healing is the journey of music

In your bones

The fabric of constellations of notes and pings
creating walruses of times inside a body
It isn't about dancing
although it is a dance

When you get *in*
Then you leave this here
Proposal we call healing

to honey
or Jupiter
to a crashed recital of *my favorite things*

Because you can't occupy the future while walking to it
YET
but you do when you've claimed that future first
then it is already gone
And you are walking somewhere it has not been

I don't really believe that you can't occupy
A future and a now simultaneously
Of course, you can

To ing a thing is to invoke a future

Heal
Ing
We go to a place that is not ever again.

I wrote this awakened from a sweat-filled colorful kaleidoscopic dream. The day before I was in a House Sermon led by the legendary performance artist, writer, and ordained minister Marvin K. White whose ceremony titled *Housemology: The Theory of Ehvurething* was exactly that: *Ehvurething*.
He deepened the slippage in the waters of House, he invited us to experience the collisions of the Praise House and sweat circle, a now internationally embraced culture started by Black gay men in Chicago in the 1980s. It was another way they were painting their lives back alive, documenting and jacking something that would live beyond the Warehouse or AIDS. Pastor White spread baby powder at the threshold of the entrances. Our footsteps created ghosts of we and us of our befores – lest we let ourselves disappear.

So I say again.
I've been dreaming in music.
And seeing in the dark.

I – in the Ifá tradition, a "+1" invokes the infinite. The next. The Yorùbá cosmology reflects an awareness that there is a world to be, a knowing of ourselves to be and an earth to become.

Quando a maré vazá
Vou ver Juliana aê
Vou ver Juliana aê
Vou ver Juliana

I sat next to Mestre. On his left sat every inch of his age present on the *bateria*. He listened to, listened in with the time at his feet, at his eyes and said, "*Canta.*"

Quando a maré vazá

I was transported to the waters I remembered of Bahia and the smells of fresh cheese grilled with oregano, skirts spinning in circles, palm leaves falling on my lap.

Vou ver Juliana aê

The sound of samba drums still echoed themselves against the Pelourinho cobblestones although we were in Harlem. And I thought of a woman.

Not only flesh, but too, a place. A sharpened blade.

Mestre said, "Stop." "That is a song a man sings to a woman."

Vou ver Juliana

I kept thinking to the expanse of ocean against the corner that became me in that room. A dam that walled back the tides of my sexuality and my gender.
That story, too, woke me out of a kind of sleep. In preparation for this keynote I was thinking about Black Diasporic traditions, liquid or liquidity, where we have met each other. And the far too plentiful experiences of boulders and rough edges. I searched for another proposal.
Something fluid but not liquid. A Blackness with flow, yet free from water scenarios that position our conditions with drownings, murderous submerges, or the ocean nightmare of our way to Diaspora. The flow that honors transformation, the fluidity of the ocean floor shapeshifting to galactic space. Where Blackness births things.

II – One and One as One and Two, The Sacred Twins, Ibeji. The force of two as one, enfleshed and spirit. We/Us.
I'm going to talk to you about the dark.[1]

1929 The United States began its withdrawal from Haiti.[2] By 1934 they officially withdrew, yet its occupation had succeeded in creating lasting economic dependence *and* enduring imperial presence.

1930 The Carnegie Corporation initiated a study on poverty entitled: *The Commission on the Poor White Problem in South Africa*.[3] The study was published in 1932 and became a foundation for the apartheid project. The recommendations this study made to address white poverty included to segregate and delegate Black labor, along with directly taking land from Blacks to give to white farmers.

1932 Thomas Dorsey after losing his wife and newborn child authored "Take My Hand, Precious Lord."[4]

In 1932 the 40-year Tuskegee assault, concocted by the U.S. Public Health Service (with support from the American Medical Association and National Medical Association) began. 600 Black men were told they were being treated for "bad blood," 399 were given syphilis, 201 were given nothing. Neither group received actual treatment for their real illnesses, nor the disease inflicted upon them.

In 1933 there were 28 reported lynchings in the U.S.[5] 28 sorrows, missings. 28 times that white people dressed up and took photographs next to bodies as bonfires, or put on hoods, or simply stepped out of doors. 28 times that we know.

In 1933 Dark matter made itself known.

Dark matter wasn't discovered. Its unconcealment was calculated in response to global, accumulated attempts at Black erasure. Dark matter is invisible, indirectly observable, yet undeniably there.
The astrophysicist who discovered a mass in 1933, having more volume than could be explained by its luminosity, noted an "unseen mass," dark matter. This unseen "there" was the only possible explanation. Its counterpart, dark energy, was unconcealed in 1998 and even less is known about it beyond the fact that it repels gravity and affects the rate at which the universe expands.

Recently scientists have hypothesized that these two forces may not be two different elements at all, an invisible 96% percent co-composing the universe, but one dark "superfluid," an extremely cold substance with negative mass.[6]

Dark matter and dark energy exemplify the great what ifs? They say simply, "no thank you" to and defy binary classification demanding that language be invented, that imaginations and realities be stretched or abandoned, that paradigms be dismantled from simply knowing that it is here. The inevitability of its something is the work. The *something* makes itself known regardless of a language, context, or desire to receive it. In fact, the work of trying to know or name that which is presenced will always fail. You gotta *be* with it.

#queerandtransasfuck.

"Newton and Einstein knew there was another element of the universe they couldn't explain. Newton invoked God, Einstein added lambda – the element to keep the universe from collapsing that counteracted gravity."[7]

The framework and languaging of the invisible co-compositional powers of the universe as a "dark fluid" or a "super fluid" mimics the wrought histories of scientific racism, yet, I find that they also partner many elements of Black Transembodied experientials and Black experimental performativities. Many a scholar, a poet, an artist, a homie on the block have articulated the powers of Black being and of the performativities of "the cool." *And*, I believe, there is more to it.

The dark fluid/superfluid theory is evidence that our beingness-es are old and ancient, that the dark unconceals a cosmic evidence beyond some easy balance, either-or dichotomy, as it is understood that the universe is made possible through its consistent inconsistencies of inhomogeneity. The universe, being composed mostly of a fluid invisibility, unlocks both that fluidity is at the core of what keeps gravity and our universe in check, and its invisibility suggests something of our Divine cosmologies at work. We simply know that it is because it is here doing its work.

I must make it plain that I am not suggesting that the invisibilization of any of us is something to try to make galactic or any other sense of. I *am* saying that we aren't (and neither is the superfluid) actually invisible, but that darkness is a sacred magic that requires something other than eyes, and a new seeing altogether, which Blackness has always demanded. A truth that Black Trans and Nonbinary-embodied experiences are too invoking of us.

And there is a danger when we accumulate unacknowledged invisibilities and make voids of ourselves or inside ourselves.

III – Esu
I'll return to the dark.

Hear the sound of a caixixi
– the soft percussion reminiscent
of a rain stick – a Brazilian
handheld shaker woven like
a small basket with an arched
handle that allows for the
instrument to be cupped in the
palm of the hand

The center of four intersecting lines. Surrounded by roads and directions. Cigar smoke coding the air coating the sky.
I searched the messages for more 33s. 3s. 3s. 33s. 3s. 3s. 33s.

Between January 1st, 2018 and September 30th, 2019, 331 transgender and gender diverse people were killed worldwide. Those lost to us who we could name because their gender identities were honored, and their deaths reported.[8]

130 in Brazil
63 in Mexico, 30 in the U.S.
1 plus 3, 4 plus 6, 10 plus 3, 4. 4 plus 3 is 7.

3,314 transgender and gender-diverse people were killed globally between January 1st, 2008, and September 2019.

At least 10 in the U.S. thus far in 2020.[9]

There is a danger when we accumulate unacknowledged invisibilities and make voids of ourselves or inside ourselves.

1933 (the year Dark Matter was unconcealed) – 1 plus 9, 10 plus 3 plus 3, 6. 6 plus 1 is 7. Yemanja – the great mother. Cool nourishing water and fierce protector.

caixixi
silences
hand falls
empty

To whose feet we are being called to answer to the murder of her children?
And not only in the silences but the dying from which there are no earthly returns.

We here, do not have an out.
We all, you all too, have a responsibility to save and better the lives of the Black Queer, the Black transgender and nonbinary students in your classrooms, those SuperFluid Walking Glories in your dance companies, in your auditions, in your lives. It is not enough to have trans and gender-diverse folk in the room without also disrupting the binary thinking, practices, and "traditions" that serve to further ostracize and injure.

Consider how do lines moving across the floor divided by binary genders create a liberated space for all of the bodies in it? Whose line is it anyway, if it serves to marginalize the walking glories in the room? Our traditions are not insulted by our revolutions.

Consider how binary changing rooms create spaces of potential anxiety, trauma, or violence.

Consider how heteronormative constructs of masculinity and femininity limit choreographic practices and forms, as well as performance opportunities and self-expressions.

Consider how funding, leadership, community-building, and choreographic opportunities offered to women with an asterisk are still only really invitations for cisgendered women. If transwomen and Nonbinary people assigned female at birth are not named, it cannot be assumed that the constructs that undergird those spaces themselves are in turn made safe for us.

Black trans and nonbinary, Black Queer dancers, we are too of this Diaspora – and always have been – we're here needing a space in dance that feels as Black as our skins, something that belongs to the bones like our genders and our sexualities belong to us. We are trying to live and breathe and sweat on the floor to lift we up from the 3s and 33s, the dying around us. Around the Black transwomen most vulnerable to anti-trans violence. That space in dance, too, has to be made to be as superfluid as our genders and sexualities and darkness.

Pronouns, presences, and bathrooms only begin to unconceal what is there of who we are. And we keep on naming ourselves to stay alive. Our beautiful Diasporic community is no less a continent than the land from which we were seeded. We have always been a many. Our languaging of gender in fluidities resists binaries that were never meant to hold our continents anyway, so why would we accept that somehow colonizers got gender or sexuality right but enslavement and genocide wrong?

Breathe.

IV – Super Black – 400 +1 the inifinite, a many.

I am a Black Queer Trans Nonbinary Artist, moving embodied memories of ancestors and transcestors. As elder Iya Fakayode says, "If we are, then someone else in our line was. We are not the first."

SA Smythe (very much alive): scholar, translator, poet in their forthcoming article, "Can I get a Witness? Black Feminism, Trans Embodiment, and Thriving Past the Fault Lines of Care," writes, "What does it mean for a space to be open to trans, gender nonconforming, and nonbinary folks other than just the ones we think we like or know? The problem of hypervisibility/invisibility is one that is incredibly salient for all Black people and a key feature of the antiblackness that makes this world. Black people are routinely unseen as themselves because they are seen through the metrics of threat or excess."[10]

Through whose eyes are we seeing each other? What does it mean for the Superfluid of us to actually be invited to these spaces? What does this "practice of care" entail? Is the space itself or the organizing accountables themselves challenging binary thinking and positionalities? Having Transgender and Nonbinary folk in the room is too, an invitation for us to evaluate and, if necessary, remake the room itself. But if it is a real invitation, that evaluation and labor can't wait on our arrival.

Breathe.

the Dark around you
unconceals slightly
suddenly

One of the mythologies of the caixixi is that the first one was filled with the teeth of a murdered African woman, a powerful warrior whose call to liberation persists every time this instrument is played. I think we should also consider the ways this story amplifies the ongoing, often invisible labor of Black women, and the expected laboring of the Black body even in death.
There is a danger when we don't see us. When we accumulate invisibilities and make voids of ourselves or inside ourselves.

the Dark around you
fully unconceals
it is Black

Breathe.

Now, I return to the blood.

An invitation to be in the flow. To acknowledge that shapeshifting liquidity of Blackness, which has always been anyway, is to be confronted with the ways the internalized terrors of white supremacy encourage stasis. In Eastern medicinal and spiritual traditions, blood stasis speaks to blockages of flow inside us that are caused by physical, emotional, or energetic traumas. Blood stasis causes pain, disease, dis-ease, and illness requiring us to examine every road in our lives.

Whether it be from pigeonholing our fullest explorations of "tradition" or supporting only the most "respectable" of Black performativity with our witnessing or our dollars we create a stasis in our blood. These erasures don't just resolve themselves "up there" so they can therefore be tolerated, they are ruptures here, now. Beyond and including this room, this context. Blood stasis muddies the blood memory our ancestors have gifted us along with that which we serve to pass on to our next ones. And haven't we inherited enough traumas? The embrace of our dark capacities expands the possibilities of flow to being beyond salt-watered absorption and coagulated stillness. As the dark teaches us, we were meant to move: cool, fluid, Black.

MID
NIGHT
GRO
UND
OF
FER

Take yourself outside into midnight. Place an offering on the ground. Breathe.

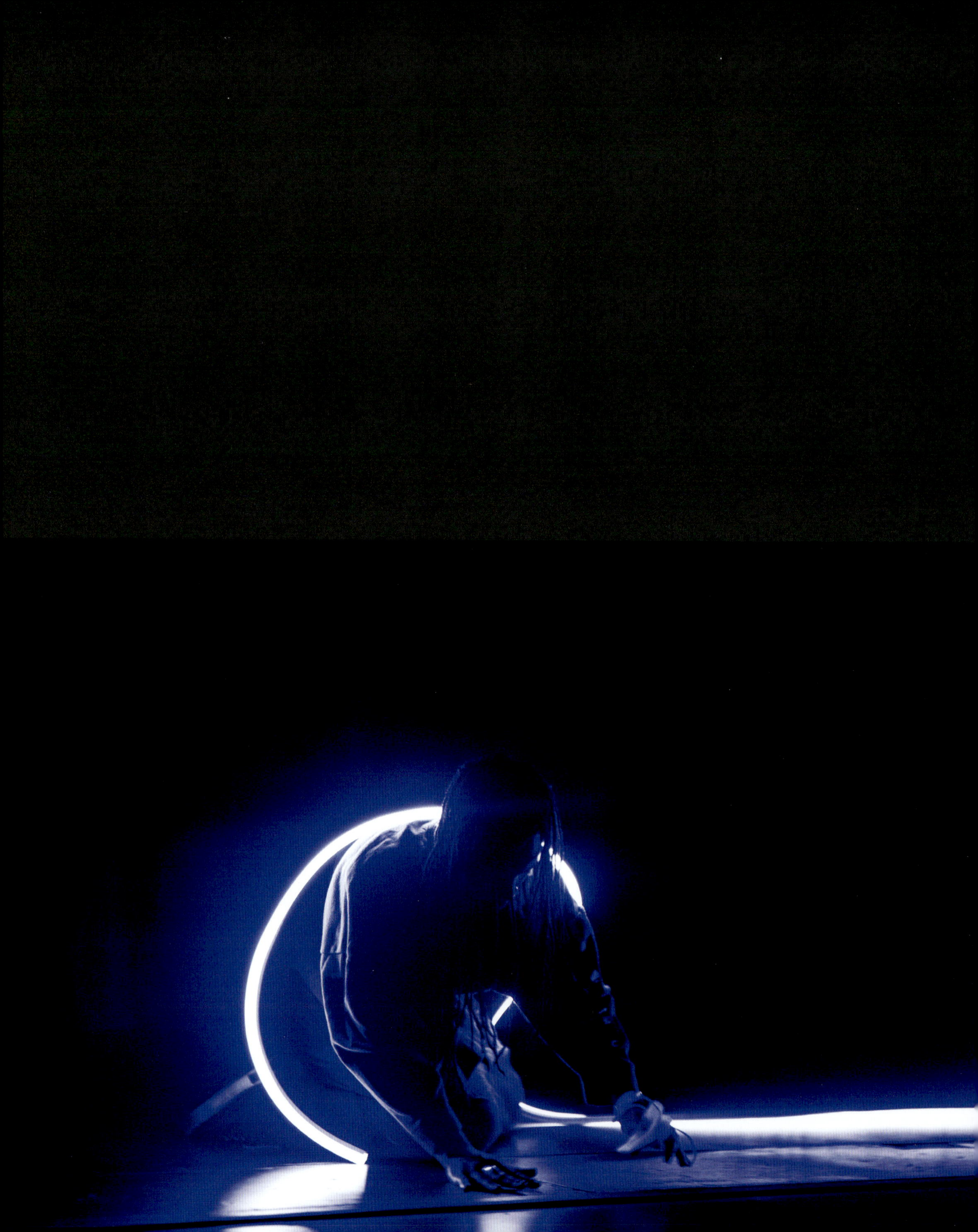

Here we are. Beyond we are.
Gratitude to all of the dear ones, elders, ancestors, comrades, kinfolk, and chosen family who hold us in our works, in our living. Gratitude for the ancestors who have called this work forth, who have tended to the lands and futures holding this work, this place, these collaborators. Us. You.
Gratitude to EMPAC, Ashley Ferro-Murray, Johannes Goebel, and the entire brilliant staff that are moving dream into manifestation. Thank you for your listening.
Here we are. Beyond we are. BREATHE
We're going to begin with gathering in the dark. I'll talk you through it and guide you through it. If you've been in a talk with me recently you've heard some version of this, it has become an important way to introduce audiences and fellow gatherers to the dark together, a short offering to collectivize in darkness as a landscape, context, and new experiential.

We begin again

Are there any Wu-Tang Clan fans in the house? The virtual house?

GZA the Genius, emcee, producer, member of the legendary Wu-Tang Clan has been working on a dark matter album for ten years. Something about time that allows for time. Something about the different ways that the sciences and disciplines like music and visual art understand and respect process. The ability to ask the same question – a question expansive enough – for a decade or a lifetime. To keep going until …
I'm starting with building a context about time that is the one I want to swim in versus what is often expected or honored in live performance.
I am creating work that requires I keep going until …

I started the research that would bring me to dark matter and dark energy in 2017, these concepts took hold and have transformed me, and in 2019 the full form of my constellation of trans/anti/beyond disciplinary art works, *The Unarrival Experiments*, unconcealed itself.
Today, I am going to share some of my out loud and developing experiences of working within emerging technologies and what has been a corporeal, liberatory, racialized, and complicated experience.

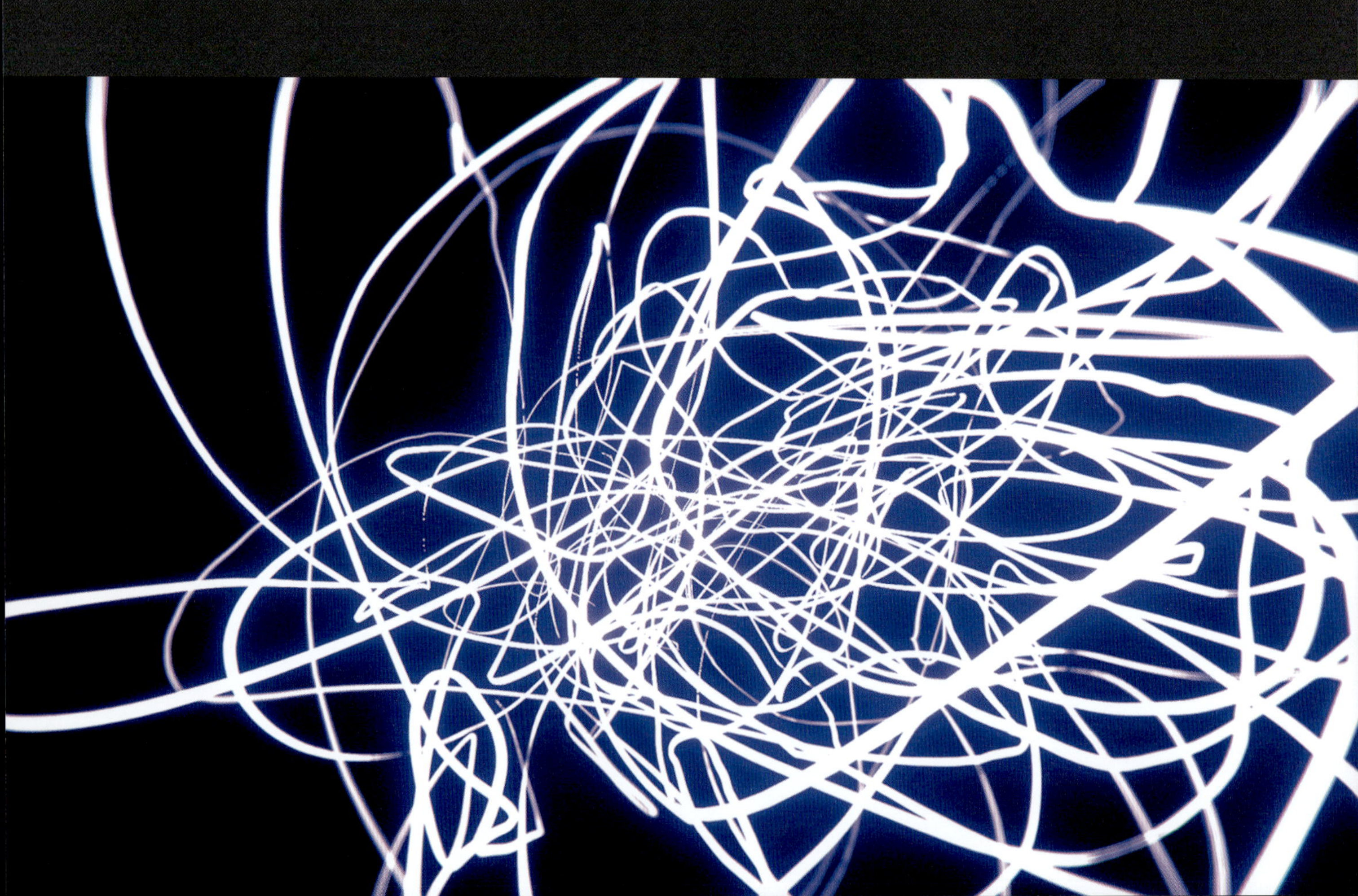

The previous page is a video still of one of the first experiences I had where I began a process of creating with preexisting VR software. Initially, I explored translation: creating VR worlds that echoed my studio-based experiments with neon flex, where I discovered the contrast with light and dark, its extreme brightness further signifying upon the darkness I had been chasing for four years. It is also a little painful to look at right now; I was so new to VR – it is messy and delightfully playful, for which I also love it. There is a sentimental archive in this video. Learning how to move with a headset as an appendage, its cord an umbilical or spinal touchpoint that limits me and makes that connection to this imaginary world possible, but is not human or organic. Not quite yet breathing.

My body provides the necessary inhalation to activate what is animated inside and through the headset. This digital/human/alien-esque symbiosis and the potentiality of the VR experience being a fully embodied one is what keeps me inside it.

Before I go deeper into this work, I want to rewind to discuss a project I created before *The Unarrival Experiments* to share some of the technological world and ideas that opened a portal into this one.

Oba Qween Baba King Baba premiered in 2019 at Danspace Project at St. Marks Church in New York City. My incredible team included Tuçe Yasak in lighting, A.J. McClenon in music, Gil Sperling in video and projections, performers Kirsten Davis, Paloma McGregor, and Shayla Vie Jenkins and myself, and featured giants in theatre, music, and art Djola Branner and Douglas R. Ewart.

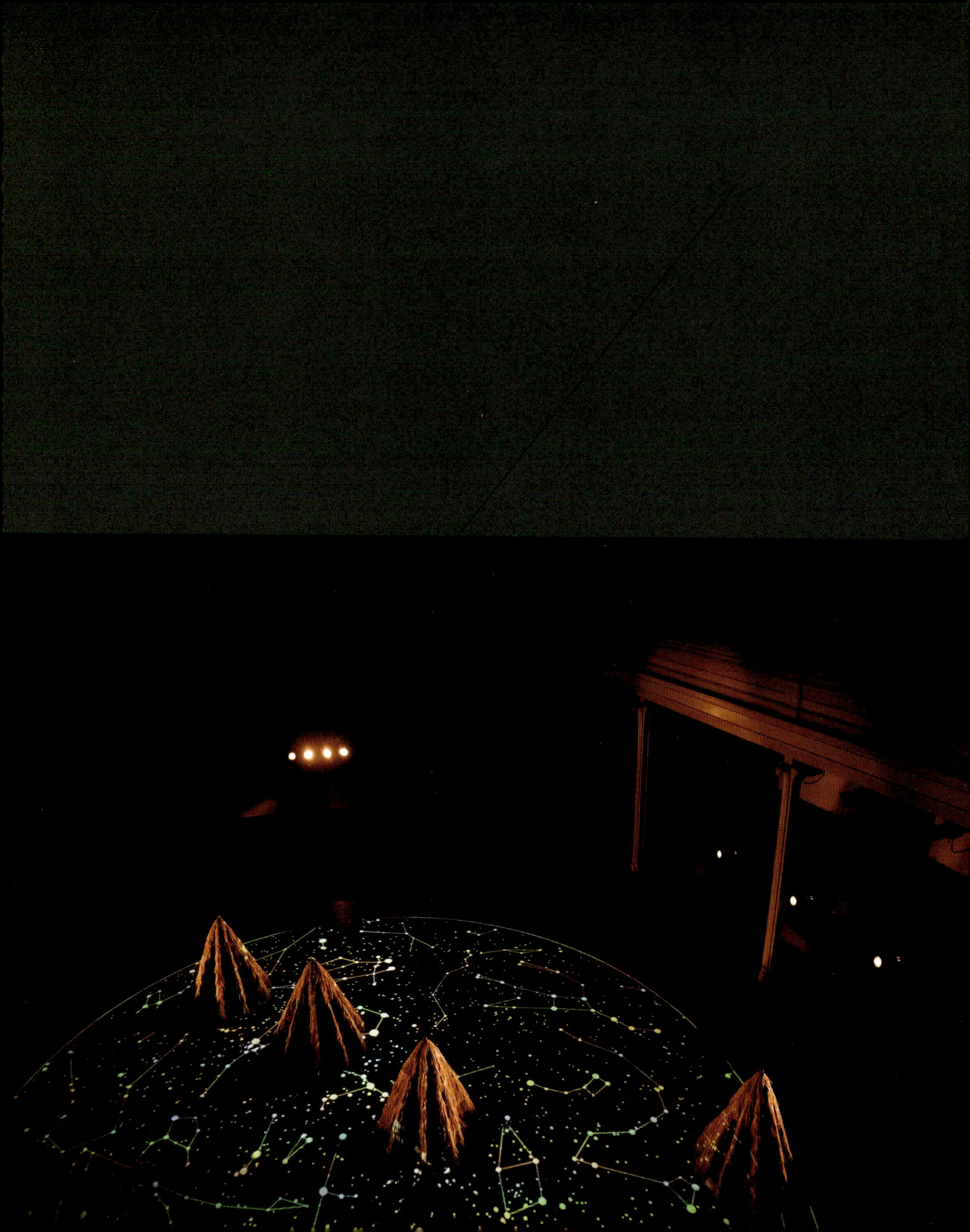

Oba Qween Baba King Baba traces Queerness in the Divine of Black spiritual lineages and is designed to be seen from above, bringing the cosmos to the floor as well as the sky. It is a sibling project to *The Unarrival Experiments*, queering free ancient technologics. One of the key innovations of this work was enabling the performance to be seen from above, a design I conceived to reimagine the "slave gallery" – historically a second-story viewing space constructed to segregate enslaved congregants considered unworthy of the sanctuary – as a throne, the honored seat and sightline. Additionally, I recontextualized Órísá rhythms and iconography in the performance, costume, and object work to highlight the ways in which queer embodiments of the past, the now, and possible futures were already notably present.

What was unlocked here, and that remain the important in the workings of technology/technologies and science in my art practices, are the connections between African Indigenous thoughts, symbologies, and systems, quantum time and field theories, and embodiment: the heart, the movement, the live or lived experiential.

Why VR and dark matter and dark energy? Why this technology with a work about "unarriving," cosmic darkness, and invisibility as technology?

I turned to VR initially because I knew that I was working within realms of thought and creative world-making that were challenging, perhaps paradigm shifting, and fantastical. I needed a place where being in an imaginary was its very platform, so that the rules of my human experiential could be bent, played with, manipulated at my command. VR offered that kind of simultaneity, the yes/and of being within my body and not (much like I experience gender), of being of this time and not. It allows me a quantum experience, surreal.

And, there is something very queered/queer-like about the experience of the fantastical in VR. A sort of "drag" performance on reality. One can become or inhabit, free climb mountains, travel space, or sit upon the ocean floor. All without moving your feet – which undergirds some of the challenges.

In my work at EMPAC, as part of *The Unarrival Experiments*, we are building what is titled *Transtraterrestiral*, and the conduction of what I am calling an *Unconcealment Ceremony*: a score or ritual series or alien-transmitted archive where I will be asking "How do virtual reality technologies in partnership with and controlled by Black Queer and Trans artists speak to and invoke a universe where their lives are not endangered?," "What does an activated, collectivized darkness unconceal?," "What are the dimensions of internal, external, and racialized darkness?" In order to cultivate a care-centered and rigorously considered, technologically capable space, we have started with a prototype.

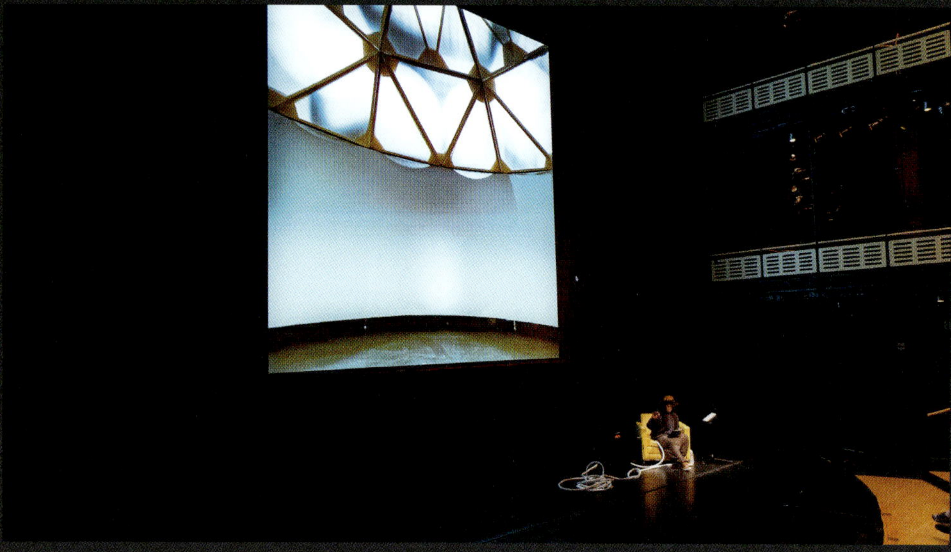

This "half dome" prototype has been engineered and assembled by the phenomenal team here at EMPAC to support my research and to inform the final design of the dome|space|ship, the architectural home and the transportation device for the world of the work. One of the stories and lead voices in *The Unarrival Experiments* is a genderless, bodyless ancestor who is the caretaker of the first home in the sky for Black Trans people. The dome is the first *egbe*, the first home, and functions as the vehicle within which traveling thereto is possible. Its fuel, function, collaborator, driver, is the dark. The dome is a spaceship and a geography.

The dome also became necessary because of relentless intervention of white and light in every environment where I attempted to research and develop the work. Seeing, in an ableist and spectacalized framework, have made it impossible in nearly every space in the world I have visited to experience deep darkness. What I am after in this world and in VR is to silence the light. To co-create a world where it is an aberration, the experiential of the theoretical, metaphysical articulations of dark, darkness, and blackness.

The challenge with this work is for me to achieve the yes/and. The ability to experience a deep, uninterrupted darkness *and* have moments of vibrant, inspired VR projection. And to do so by eliminating the factors that conventionally make that possible (lighter-colored or white projection surfaces). Shifting to darkness as the air and the walls recondition the needs of seeing toward a reworking of how light and projections can be experienced or created in order to prioritize the dark while not losing, when desired, rich projected imagery.

It's a tall order.

But if we can do this, if we can get witnesses and ourselves to appreciate the richness of darkness, I believe that it can reconfigure how Blackness is experienced, respected, honored, and valued on this plane for now and for the next. There is no doubt, and there is evidence in the cosmos, in Indigenous thinking across Diaspora, that the darkness is necessary. And that it exists beyond a colonial counterpoint to whiteness or good.

Here I lean to and am reminded of the problematics of the fact that the technologies are often developed by and within a context that is ableist, antiblack and antiIndigenous, that is homophobic and transphobic, steeped in cisheteronormativity, patriarchy, and white supremacy. That is not likely a surprise to the folks here. Gaming and technology communities along with the sciences exist in our global reality of that ism and ic list, so unfortunately, VR, while capable of so much is often conditioned by the limitations of human trash.

It is also the reason why it is vital that criticality be a part of the teaching, training, and development of these technologies. Otherwise folks take their earthly pains and hates along with them into the digital, technological, and virtual realm.

Avatars act as digital masks where white hoods grip light sabers and adorn themselves in digital phosphorescent facsimiles. When I enter a community room or seek out metaverses, my Blackness does not disappear behind the goggles. The anonymity of avatars does not equalize. Conversely, vulnerabilities abound and I find myself desperate to connect with BIPOC QTs there.

The idea that this kind of technology and others, AI and all of the algorithmic technologies to be, will remain in the hands primarily of people who seek to replicate the worst versions of humanity in a metaverse is terrifying. But it is what is happening.

Metaverses/VR gathering rooms can be rife with unwanted sexual contact and content, hate speech and attacks. The more "real" these technologies become the more "real" their impact on our bodies, our psyches, and our imaginations.

It is meaningful in the moment it happens, and upon the future of the spirit and brain of the person who enters into a space presented as a magical unknown someplace, only to have the corporeal and emotional familiarities of human violence acted upon them.

I refuse that. And ask, what is the math of a liberatory code? Of liberatory coding?

While I assert that it is critical that Black and Queer and Trans folks create, develop, and participate in these technologies, I think it is important that we do so with thoughtful analysis, because without it, we allow ourselves to be duped into participating in the Black global genocidal erasure project. VR and AI are versions of a reality where, like the internet, anonymity allows for magic as well

as mayhem. We should be cautious of any space that thrives in the erasures of our bodies and the multiple expressions of corporeality.

I think to Nnedi Okorafor who in *Who Fears Death* introduces a future where the remaining technology will be that of the Black body, spiritually tooled and armored with otherworldly abilities. I see in my mind's eye, lifted from those pages, sand-dusted stretches of computers as discards. Imagining a future where digital technology is obsolete at best, inferior to that embodied by humans at least. It is a deeply spiritual and indigenous understanding of futurity and technology.

And it does feel real, and often possible, in VR.

One of the proposals for my working has been to focus on the spaces where I am the most fully embodied, where I can develop content inside the technology utilizing physicality as a collaborator, beyond and maybe rudimentarily, I explore what my body makes of and with the tech. Because while the "real" of VR is not, if it is good one's body is tricked by the mind into believing something has happened that has not. One's nervous system responds, heart rate can increase, fight or flight responses triggered in addition to the joys, the laughter, the wonderment that is possible. I am finding that when my body is involved, it can handle the "real/unreal" of the nervous system responses, as I can delineate more clearly where I am, who I am, and what is happening. This kind of being in the tech is also a way to consider a trauma-informed relationship to the technology.

When I started in VR I thought immediately about how it is a tool for dreaming. It is literally a projection of the imaginary, and straight white men cannot be the keepers of dreaming Black futures. Every time I pick up a headset, I think about my childself in a room with books and puzzles, making a world, pretending, journeying somewhere beyond through play. So much of that I had to do myself, and find on my own. A part of why creating within the tech appeals to me and I think is important is because it supports unboundedness (to the extent of the software) to create *within* the fantastical. It is also why coders, designers, and consumers of a multitude of experiences and those who will approach technology with sensitive, trauma-informed, and decolonial lenses, must be supported.

I want to leave you by saying the names of a few Black science fiction and speculative fiction writers who are women and nonbinary folk and who are dreamers that trace the fantastical with and within a Black embodied possibility: Nnedi Okorafor, Tananareve Due, Octavia E. Butler, NK Jemisin, Alexis Pauline Gumbs, Black Quantum Futurism, and Nalo Hopkinson.

Thank you.

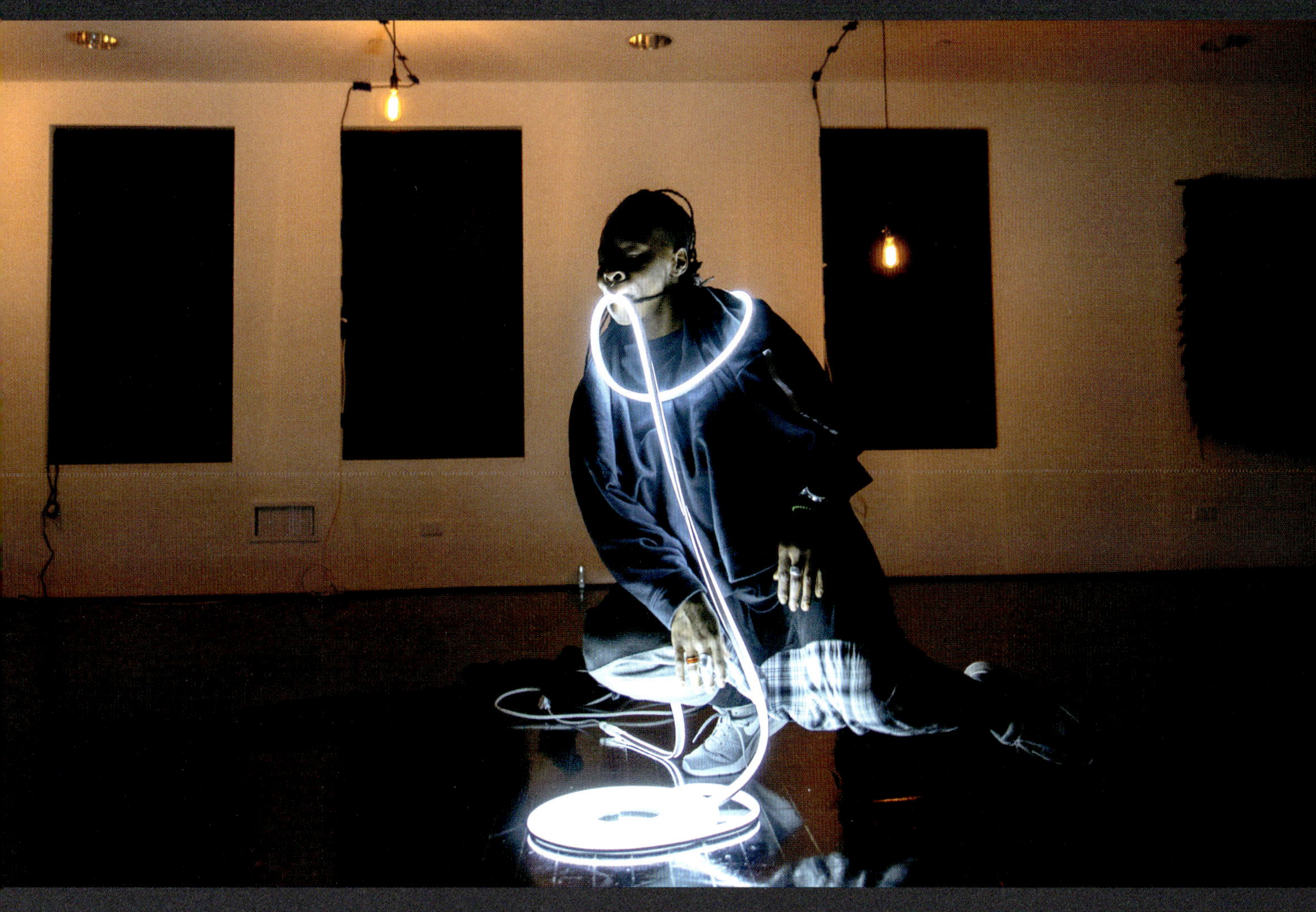

I danced in a dark hole and become drunk
A memory I never had

cobblestone pathways form to mars from one of my future fleshes

same sky between two waters
between two waters
at the same time i
the and of a storm

sun lost but not really not ever
celestial blue interrupted by clouds in strokes
cotton candy pulled apart between palms
the kind of cluster my ancestor may have loved before
being forced to pick it
bloody and rough up their fingers

Oya and Yemoja dance the storm as a blues

dark matte azure protrusion of mists
celebrate themselves by
passing slowly by
intervene on the spell of the air

It was drenched in blue
after hours
liquor
youth percolating
Ohio skins steel
condensation
red flame scatter pathways
at their feet
queer
proselytizing against the floors
of their father's emptied factories i

could still smell the smoke

"tell me again …"
usher & little john
and two women
in front of me
moving pussy
grind thighs and thick
against each other
blessing the room with want

it was somewhere around 3am
i was 19
or
20

then the music changed

a familiar gathering ensued
all the people
in one direction
in lines
getting ready for unison

"be careful, this one gets really fast."

the Detroit hustle
in Cleveland danced to Plastic Dreams
at the hands of a Dutch producer dance music

made ~~popular~~
made possible
made
by Black queer
folks lifting
selves in sweat
i am not sure
we were aware
in that midwest
moment
how queer it all was

the flash of it all
moisture and prayer
increase in beats
per minute
until
our quarter turns
split us into
a shout
repetition and trance
bass and laughter among strangers
we were
suddenly all on the same fucking step
in time
it's a spiritual convening
Black people do
in a particular kind of way
it is not enough
to do the steps
or simply to know
them
you gotta move
them
absorb
them
but only enough to stir the bottom
without spilling the mix over the top
keep
what's wild
on

and in the center of the heat
so it can swell

more

in the midwest
line dances are serious business

and if it aint to you
you learn
to get the fuck out the way

Some call it a shuffle.
or hustle.
Depending on where go
your feet.
But what we are doing
is line dancing.

Moving lines
in the logic of the Kongo Cosmogram.

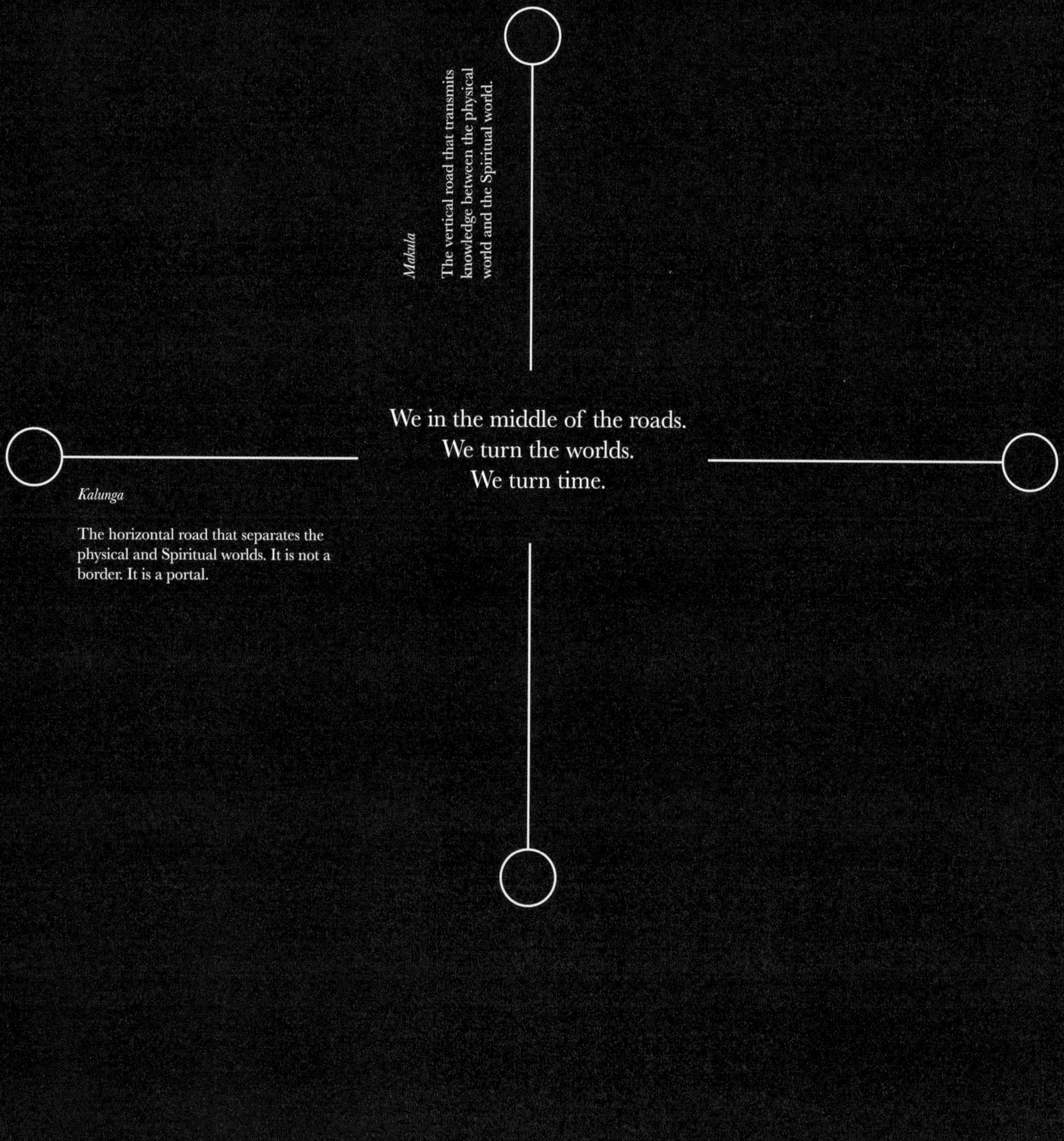

Makula

The vertical road that transmits knowledge between the physical world and the Spiritual world.

We in the middle of the roads.
We turn the worlds.
We turn time.

Kalunga

The horizontal road that separates the physical and Spiritual worlds. It is not a border. It is a portal.

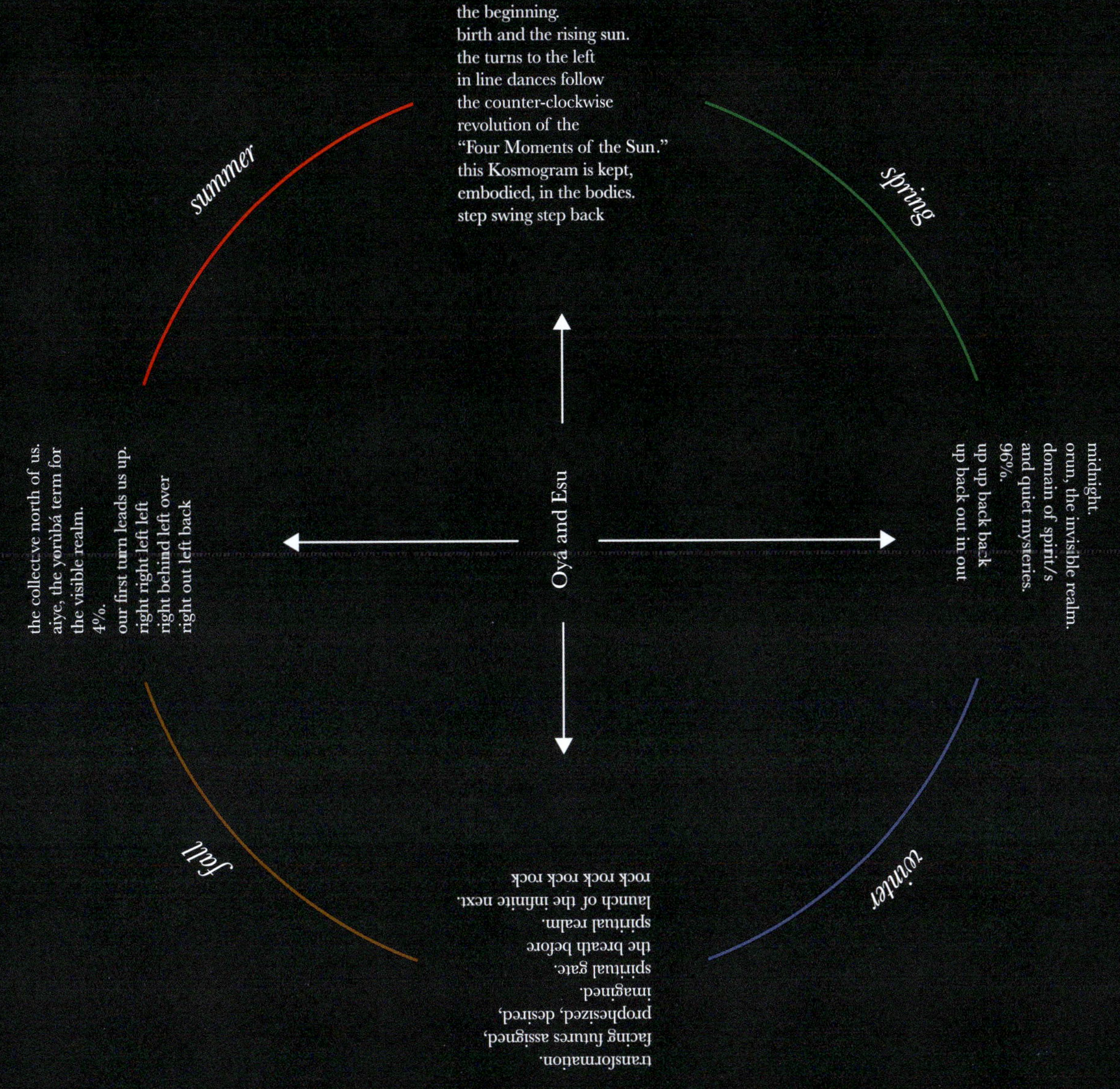
the beginning.
birth and the rising sun.
the turns to the left
in line dances follow
the counter-clockwise
revolution of the
"Four Moments of the Sun."
this Kosmogram is kept,
embodied, in the bodies.
step swing step back
summer
spring
Oyá and Esu
the collective north of us.
aiye, the yorùbá term for
the visible realm.
4%.
our first turn leads us up.
right right left left
right behind left over
right out left back
midnight.
orun, the invisible realm.
domain of spirit/s
and quiet mysteries.
96%.
up up back back
up back out in out
fall
winter
transformation.
facing futures assigned,
prophesized, desired,
imagined.
spiritual gate.
the breath before
spiritual realm.
launch of the infinite next.
rock rock rock rock

the Kongo Cosmogram articulates
by the BaKongo peoples of central
an understanding of cyclic time that
indigenous African cosmologies.
the ways that Black sociality is
multiple in its embodiments across
migrations. Circular time is old and
intrusions that fashion our Black
beyond anti-clockwise, as neither
ever "clockwise."

we move the
crossroads
as we turn.

while our feet
navigate on
one plane,
we activate
multiples
around us.

a sphere
rather than
circle.

every stepper
a contribution
to the shape
shifting in this
time traveling
practice.

time as conceptualized and practiced
Africa. Its sacred temporality charts is
is shared across many other
My exploration of it seeks to expose
queered, spiritual, ancient, and
oceanic tragedies and bipedal
already always antithetical to linear
spheres into white lines. We are
our time, nor us as timekeepers were

Anchored in the west, the sunset position is ruled by Oyá,
who supports transitions to the ancestral plane, keeper of cemeteries, of the gates.
Bringer of change.

Sunset is an alchemical threshold.

With Oyá, Agayu sits at the number 9.
Agayu supports journeys fraught with obstacles.
A mover of impossibility.
The line dance, as a migration, calls in the keeper of the wilderness,
sun, river, and volcano.

like a group of
drummers,
calling to the
gods, there are
multiple ways
the rhythm is
embodied: the
basic stepper;
cool, easy; the
one always
ready to teach;
the stepper
who is all flair;
it is all done
with such
style, skill, and
always on the
downbeat.
It's real Black

Esu grounds the east, opens pathways, roads, and doors. Mover of messages between the Spirit and physical worlds. Keeper of the crossroads.

Represented by the color black, it is the functional and metaphysical beginning.

Sunrise opens.

Hey Lei,
What did you do, to make a mark on this world?
What mountains did you climb?
Which angels gave you their wings?
Which skies have you flown?
When you reached the heavens, who was there to catch you when you fell?
And did they tell you that you saved them too, like you saved me?
That they are mending their wings and holding them up to the sun, just to step back and watch you fly.
So go ahead, Lei: fly.

Hey Lei

Leti meets the camera lens sitting alone in a church pew. The congregation is introduced on their feet. Sunday's best from head to toe. Colors fill the room around Leti, and she, stoic and still, in white. Her black hat with white stripes takes up the space she won't/doesn't.

There is a pause after "Lei" as the camera zooms in, a breath and body we don't see.

*

In the Nike "Be True" campaign of 2017, the commercial from which this text is lifted, legendary vogue dancer and trans icon of Afro-Puerto Rican descent twirls on a quiet New York street painted in the deep blue haze of sunset. She walks in percussion while her arms push forward in time and in opposition to her steps. As she turns, her orange jacket is caught by air revealing a white sports bra with black trim and white pants.

Hers is the disappeared body for whom this text is penned.

What did you do to make a mark on this world?
What mountains did you climb?
Which angels gave you their wings?

A close-up of Leiomy's face on the right side of the frame, eyes closed, chin slightly pointed down. Sweat and heat make a blur of the lens. She seems to breathe for us.

"I think we are the flesh of what quantum mechanics is discovering" – Ashon Crawley, *The Lonely Letters*

"we": we Black queer folk. Those moving blackqueer spacetime in breath and being.
A spacetime that is nonlinear, anti-normative.
"we": the gatekeepers.

Sobonfu E. Somé in *The Spirit of Intimacy: Ancient Teaching in the Ways of Relationships* articulates that in Dagara culture there is no word for "gay" or "lesbian," that they are understood as gatekeepers, beings that connect the village to the Spirit world. In Dagara culture there are two types of gatekeepers, those within the Dagara system of cosmology, the keepers of precise gates, water, earth, fire, mineral, or earth. The second group's domain is the entire Spirit world, those who exist in both the earthly plane and the Spirit world. Queer people are those gatekeepers.[1]

I am interested in the relationship between quantum theory, imagination, and Spirit/uality. The ways in which Black and Indigenous queer and transgender people are keepers of time and our movement through it. The use of ritualized African indigenous spirituality throughout *Lovecraft* necessarily complicates the employ of "magic" beyond colonized relegations to the demonic, particularly because it is intertwined with quantum theory and multidimensionality at the point where Spirit/uality and symbology invoke the movement across planes. Queer folk and transgender folk are keepers of that choreography.

So, what then, are we left with when the queer and transgender keepers are diminished or disappeared in an articulation of a magical Black future or of a Black imaginary?

In episode 3, "Holy Ghost," this diminishment is most apparent because of the ways that it is so clearly an experiment in exposing Black and African Indigenous ritual as precursors of contemporary research within quantum field theory, while also going further to position ritual, performativity/embodiments, and magics as portals to Black futurity. However, this is done by absenting Black queer and transgender folk.

The camera cuts to Leiomy in a dance studio, first alone beaming a strut, then in front of a group in unision, duckwalking and hand dancing.
They move.

The scene changes to a quick outdoors shot of Leiomy sprinting down the street, again at dusk, with the faint sound of her shoes catching the pavement and pushing her body forward. She outruns the lens which shifts to an unplaceable darkened space and Leiomy filling the misty room and single warm yellow light with her arms that trace her body then the space around her.
The camera is made a partner by arching up and forward, zooming in then back and out.

*

In the Lovecraft church the camera cuts to a wide overhead view from the rear. Leti is invisibilized by the swell of claps and stamps, and the fact that she remains seated, in pause. At the first pew, 3 church mothers form a semi-circle with their arms outstretched, ready to catch or nurture a parishioner carried over in dance by spirit. She is in a shout waving her hands, repeatedly lifting then stamping her right foot, movement that shuffles her body to the left. With closed but seeing eyes she turns to run briefly down the aisle, jumps and clenches her fists.

Leti watches. Her emotions anchor to the wooden seat underneath her body and make distance of her eyes.

Which skies have you flown?
When you reached the heavens,

The camera moves forward and down and zooms in toward the space made quiet by Leti's stilling contemplation.

*

Leiomy walks down her New York street with the camera at her back zoomed in at her left shoulder, then a cut to Leiomy, now inside among a crowd. We see Precious Ebony – iconic vogue commentator and performer who voices the poem in both versions – on the mic. The room is filled with young black and brown smiles, points, feet stomping the floor in time.

Shapeshifting & Invocation.

The episode tells the story of one ceremony: the Spiritual eviction of Hiram Epstein (follower of Horatio Winthrop, founding member of the Sons of Adam and banished thief of the Book of Name's elusive missing pages) from the Winthrop home.

The ceremony begins with an invocation performed by Precious Ebony, a masterful commentator in the Ballroom/House scene. Leiomy Maldonado is disappeared. Precious is disappeared. The queer and trans people as people are rendered unnecessary, minimized to the reductive efficacy of their labors. They are instrumentalized to catalyze the spiritual work. Their sacredness acknowledged only enough to be exploited.

The word(s) throughout the series are time-travelling devices. In *Holy Ghost* a church service in 1955 and subsequent exorcism is activated by voice and beings from 2017. It can be trivialized as a simple voiceover cinematic device, but, in a series that journeys magics and futurity, it cannot be overlooked.

"You're not real. If you were you'd have some status among the nations of the world. So we're both myths." Episode 7 is visited by the words of Sun Ra (1974). What we do not hear, is the next line, and perhaps the most significant: "I do not come to you as a reality; I come to you as a myth. Because that's what black people are. Myths. I came from a dream that the black man dreamed long ago. I'm actually a present sent to you by your ancestors." If we are to take this as true, the past/future word as a truth, even more is revealed about the role of transgender people as time travelers, shapeshifters, gatekeepers.
We come as myths and as presents sent by the ancestors.

Precious and Leiomy are not real. They are a gifted mythologized presence from the future.

The read here is that as gatekeepers and holders of shapeshifting technology, Black transgender people as keepers and facilitators are necessary and invaluable to Black and African Indigenous ritual as well as Black futurity.

Who was there to catch you when you fell?
And did they tell you that you saved them too, like you saved me?

Leiomy spins then dips.
She dips again in the dance studio with younger dancers.

*

Camera at the back of the church shouter, we see a glimpse of one of the church mothers, arms still open, ready. Her gaze steady.

A cut to Leti, in whose eyes are seen the ghosted outline of the movement surrounding her in the church; they begin to make a river.
Her bottom lip trembles. She blinks.
She swallows an exhale, then tender timid rocks the shoulders and head.

That they are mending their wings and holding them up to the sun, just to step back and watch you fly.

Hands clap, hands clap, hands clap, hands clap, hands clap. Body swings in shout. Choir calls in song we cannot hear and beats a tambourine. Body swirls in a counter-clockwise circle, jogs, then jumps with arms stretched high in a v, mouth agape.

*

Outside against a grey graffiti wall a young Black dancer leans and makes precise circles and shapes of their hands. Leiomy, back in her orange jacket, smiling and laughing bouncing in joy down the street.
Leiomy and dancers in the studio. They all stand at a ballet barre in the center of the room, Leiomy leans against it in front, the others behind. All eyes and heads toward the ground. They look up at the camera in union. Leiomy lifts confidently to her feet and strides forward.
A shot in reverse of Leiomy dipping. She spins from the ground of the studio while her hair cyclones in tandem. She jumps left foot then right.

However, when Black trans people as a whole are disappeared from a Black future project – but our technologies and ancient roles are not – audiences are left with a teaching that transgender we don't need to be seen or even acknowledged as real for our work to work. That the mythologies about or that which come through us is enough to viably supplant our actual or mythological presences. This is not only false, but also dangerous.

A glaring aberration is that of Yahima Maraokoti, a Native (Arawak speaking), intersex, imprisoned keeper of the missing pages (episode 4). Yahima, rather than being disappeared or not seen, is overly exposed. We are introduced to Yahima naked, fully frontal, made a radical other. After the pages are recovered and Yahima "rescued," they return to Leti's house only to have Yahima's throat cut by Montrose. Yahima lives then dies after a total of only 12 minutes on screen. Their inclusion serves to first display then nearly immediately eliminate any presence of nonbinary genderedness and to feign an intersectional indigenous legitimacy to the narrative. What remains is that Yahima, as nonbinary, maintains the role of the keeper of a sacred mythologic, but killed off in order to recenter the binary story and Tic's place as the "good" agent of magic. The murder of Yahima by Montrose is not a fantastical story, in fact; the painful reality is that nonbinary and transgender people of color are assaulted and killed by Black men at increasing and alarming rates.

It is complex, but not mythology.

*

*

*

*

*

An intervention by Malidoma Somé is useful here. In *The Healing Wisdom of Africa: Finding Life Purpose Through Nature, Ritual, and Community*, Somé connects Black imaginary, Spirituality and quantum time. He says of Dagara,

The ceremony.

"Restless souls trapped in my house with their killer. They want out."

- (Leti, Episode 3)

Somé refers to it as a radical ritual.

"The cycle of life and death is something so engrained in us that dying at some point intersects with living, and living intersects with dying. So that when one dies, there is always the desire that that death be connected with something grand, something big. It is as if exiting this world also means entering another world where a huge welcoming committee is waiting for you … this is the reason why among Dagara people, death always calls attention to a tremendous, intense radical ritual …"[3]

Somé offers that our imagination in indigenous thinking materializes our connections to Spirit, which, by extension of queer people as gatekeepers thereto, is a manifestation of blackqueer time. The beauty of Lovecraft Country, and certainly a part of its appeal to me, is just these intersections. But the borrowing, bloodying, and bailing of queerness and transness works against the very components on which the magics are grounded (and that which make it so compelling).

Dagara cosmology teaches that queer and transgender pe are not symbols or mere evidence of the presence of spiri we make the work of spirit happen.

The house.

A well worked and dust burdened spider web claims a foyer corner. A healthy black arachnid labors. Yellow light spills upon the stairs. Cracks dissect the boarded windows, allow for sun to cheat its way inside. It is dark. Ish. Displays the sum of time and empty.

Between its walls and in its air are the unrested spirits of 8 Black South Side Chicago residents, tortured and murdered by Hiram Epstein. He mutilated them; decapitated the head of a baby and reattached it onto the looming height of a basketball player, he removed forearms and breasts, he placed adult arms on youth,

he impaled bodies with nails and metal spikes, he tore babies from wombs. Given the time (1955), history teaches that many of these types of experiments were inflicted upon Black people by white doctors without anesthesia. So we are to also understand that along with their dismemberments and sorrow amassed in the corners of the home (and with Epstein's ghost) is their pain. Perhaps enragement. Leti seeks to remove what is left unattended, and that endangers them all.

Several rituals and sacred symbols lead up to the exorcism. They also speak to the intersections of Indigenous and Black Christian spirituality that complicate and move the series. For instance, the episode opens in a church, but ends in an indigenous spiritual expelling ritual conducted by a priestess. And although a church informs the initial cinematic moments of "Holy Ghost," there are no crosses. The sanctuary has unmarked, bare, white walls. The only crosses visible are those made by the open arms of the church mothers; they in their white gloves embody the sacred shape of Jesus' cross, with the Blood of Christ signified in the choir's red robes. The crosses that are shared come most notably in two moments: a burning cross on Leti's lawn, interrupting the boarding house celebration and further announcing her white neighbor's disdain for all of their presences, and secondly, in blood upon Leti's head.

these walking glories

go
migration
move
body not place
bodies that migrate
but not place
places not
going with Them that
choose
to go
in
gender
in
body

Metamorphosis.

Black transgender embodiedness is a part of the lineage of Black and African ancestors that chose migration against the horrors and racialized reductions of the South, or of those who chose the salt water of the ocean or flights in the air back home against enslavement. Living into transness as Black people is a manifestation of the alterability of home, of place, of geographic relationality. More importantly, Black transness is both an expression of dreaming, imagining, and manifesting a many-ed self into being. This is quantum being, future-making, liberatory ritual praxis.

And shit. it is also simply survival.

Gender migration
body
transmigrates
a Land
anchors to place
grabbing at
the ankles of those
who audacity
freedom

like their Peoples
did
like their Great
Befores

Who walked
cried across
imaginary
l i n e s

making Free
making Live

or risk dissolved
self in boundaries of unrequited
biology

Babies

who in the eyes of the stayers

shoulda been broke necked at the
sight of them

chose to get up

go

to live instead of die in suffocation

or stay naked brown footed on their
mothers land

holding handles of wooden tools

The folk that stayed

Black trans embodiedness is quantum time in blood and bones: moving, in process. To be a Black transgender person is to move quantum time trickled across you in a spiritual expression of imagination. An ancestor's prayer, a time traveler, a transmogrifier, and as Somé has articulated, a gatekeeper (or as I like to say portal keeper) of those domains.

"In Blackness and the Trouble of Trans Visibility," Che Gossett tells us that "Blackness ruptures trans representability, respectability, and visibility. The grammar of 'cisgender' lacks the explanatory power to account for the colonial and anti-Black foundation violence of slavery and settler colonialism through which the gender and sex binary were forcibly rendered."[4] In short, "Blackness troubles trans/gender; blackness is trans/gender trouble."[5]

This complication pervades *Lovecraft*. As much as the magical potions and spells create pathways for transformation for the Black characters, these transformations remain within their binary gender assignments, a curious limitation. Similarly, Hiram Epstein's experiments in "Holy Ghost" propounds transformation of the Black body as a monstrous extension of white imaginary. So, "[w]ho gets to assume a body? Who gets to assume the integrity and security of that body?"[6]

For Ruby, in episode 5, "Strange Case," shapeshifting for her comes as painful, brutal. Bones break, skin peels away, blood splatters, eyes roll, all of which is accompanied by the raucous music of her screaming. She becomes white. She describes it as "being unmade."

In this episode queerness and queered bodiedness is the most visibilized. It is also the site of intense, and intensely sexualized, violence.

in home

stayed

in place

with doctrines

that survived the plagues

stayed and died on over

thumbed pages

In the word
In the gospels
In the belt

where those who never left

root and punish

those who did not leave their fathers

bourbon streets

or plantation

r o w s

instead offered

back given names.

The curses of cotton

taught the stayers to kill

those who refused place

stayed to instruct

the others that their body

belongs and does not

A subplot in this episode is built around Montrose and his secreted partner, Sammy. Montrose enters Sammy's home without a word, unbuttons his pants, bends him over and fucks him. It is fast and rough. Montrose seems to hurt Sammy; there is no exchange of intimacy. Frank Ocean's "Bad Religion" plays above their grunts:

> "If it brings me to my knees
> It's a bad religion
> This unrequited love
> To me, it's nothing but a one-man cult
> And cyanide in my styrofoam cup
> I can never make him love me
> Never make him love me"

Toward the end of this episode Ruby is told that the currency of magic was "unmitigated freedom," and she was encouraged to "do whatever the fuck [she] want[s]." This provocation follows Ruby's episode-long wrestling with the psychological traumas internalized through her walks in a body of and walks with white privilege as Hillary. Her culminating act is to punish her manager, a white man who she witnesses sexually assaulting a Black woman.

The soundtrack to this moment is Cardi B.'s "Bodak Yellow," the track that catapulted Cardi B. to celebrity stardom, and was the story of her own metamorphosis:
"got a bag and fixed my teeth,"
"I used to live in the P's, now it's a crib with a gate,"
"I don't dance now, I make money moves."

Hillary/Ruby meets "Mr. Manager" in his office and seduces him to gain control over his body. She has tied his wrists, unbuckled his pants, leads him around the room with his belt hooked around his neck. Hillary then makes red bottoms of her heels by violently sodomizing the manager. The potion begins to wear off, Ruby begins to emerge, mixing blood on blood. She strides out, covered in the inners/outers of Hillary.

"These is red bottoms, these is bloody shoes." Cardi B.

To move   to choose to go from place
and body
To die   if you move from one   and
not the other
To die   in the body of the always
other

To make of bloodied little ones   or
grown them
the black and brown such
To be made from the cast
-off
parts of punished
children who whistled   or grew yams
or loved or spilled joy   or took too
long
to step off the sidewalk   and   stand
in the street whose dreams escaped
the finality of their skinned   position
who spoke with too broad   too long a
backbone
who saw stardust   instead of dirty
linens

These ghosts

did not be come

for their children

to be

made more

of themselves

Not These

who hold sequined marathons
underneath   their gums
with shine   for epidermis
and jazz in the bottom of their
stockings

These walking glories

These transmigrators

The potentiality of the "bawse," #BlackGirlMagic, is dullened against Montrose's aggressive fucking of his partner, wherein the only framing of penetration is that of violence, even between partners, void of softness.
But there is a kiss.

Sammy announces to Montrose that they will perform Locusta Migratoria, a dance at a Chicago Drag Ball. I'm specifically using the pronouns "they/them" because while at this point Sammy and Montrose are visited by other femmes and the context is a Drag Ball, there are no pronouns used in the scene. In fact, the presence of drag celebrity Shangela complicates the moment. The scene most resembles historic descriptions of Finnie's Ball, known for live bands, female impersonators, and gender fluid gays and lesbians.[7]

The life cycle of locusts is described as "incomplete metamorphosis," it articulates a process where the insect's body change occurs gradually over time with no singular moment of major, profound physical shift – the opposite of how butterflies come into being. Instead of significant corporeal alteration, locusts can experience what is called a gregarious phase, a major shift from solitary to group living which can occur at any point in their life cycle.

"When rains return – producing moist soil and abundant green plants – those environmental conditions create a perfect storm: Locusts begin to produce rapidly and become even more crowded together. In these circumstances, they shift completely from their solitary lifestyle to a group lifestyle in what's called the gregarious phase. Locusts can even change color and body shape when they move into this phase. Their endurance increases and even their brains get larger."[8]

The Drag Ball is Montrose's entry into his gregarious phase, the moment where he witnesses, is witnessed upon, and change happens. Both Montrose and Sammy are met/meet themselves in this phase, Sammy is crowned and adorned with a first-place sash. Montrose smiles and spins in the club, is lifted (literally) by community, and finally, for the first time ever, he kisses Sammy. The incomplete metamorphosis through which Montrose has lived his life as gay is transformed, at least internally, in this moment.

chose to go from fam
iliar soil heated under rage
contempt uous exhaust ions of beat
en spirits in that place remember ed
murder but not free
dom killed the bodies hold ing light
holding the north in them selves

these migrating bodies

that left

that chose

to go

who learned from steps

leapt

to

take

place

in cracked

melting

distant

unknown

geographies

up

the only direction was free.

Transness activates a kind of uniquely individualized morphology, however, morphology is not always, and is not inherently, trans. Morphology as metamorphosis, shapeshifting, or transformation is all over *Lovecraft*, but shows up as decidedly cisheteronormative and erases Black queer and transness. The club is the only (brief) scene where the series gets close to an embodied Black magical queer radical while drawing from the technologies and spiritual intelligences by which queer and transgender presences are mediated. Yahima is the only nonbinary character in the series with magic, and the only other scene with Black queer or trans magic occurs without sound, without their voices, and is focused on the cisgendered character.

Montrose, in the club, is sonically uplifted by the falsetto of Moses Sumney, a Black queer recording artist. The magic made in the scene is again invoked by an invisible Black queer voice. Conversely, Christina Braithwaite escapes the binary gender shapeshifting paradigm by usurping Black queer and trans magic, an extension of her family's ongoing pursuit of magic made by Black people. In fact, by becoming William she gains access to intimacy with Ruby in order to coerce/trick/gift her the metamorphosis potion – another dangerous intervention where the "fantasy" of the story belies anti-trans hysterics, in this case the fear that trans people are tricking unsuspecting cisgender people into intimacy. Here is where Gossett's words return as instructional: Who gets to assume a body? Christina's and William's imaginary "transness" is instituted here to disturb and terrorize Blackness, while no space in the episode or series is created for a Black transness that wreaks havoc upon white terror.

The Ritual.

There is a dance in the cellar. Folds in the grey dark. There is old water, old sweat on the walls. Screams from the past hold story in the condensation. From ceiling to floor, in each ashen floor panel is a witness. The ritual is conducted by a Priestess and supported by Leti and Tic. She opens the ceremony by making a goat sacrifice, using its blood to protect the home. In blood she makes an x on either side of the door frame, then does the same on each of their foreheads.

"because the village is relatively small, there is a possibility of stopping every activity in order to give attention to the departed soul, so that this escort to the other world can translate into another escort in the other world to wherever the final destination of the dead is."[9]

Satan, we're gonna tear
Your kingdom down
Oh, Satan, we're gonna tear
Your kingdom down

You've been building your kingdom
All over this land
Satan, we're gonna tear
Your kingdom down, down

The Preachers are gonna preach
Your kingdom down
The Mothers are gonna pray
Your kingdom down
The Deacons are gonna pray
Your kingdom down

Episode 3 concludes with a radical ritual. It is missing a proper gatekeeper, but residuals of shapeshifting technologies are performed, and make for a very Black crescendo in the episode. Leti and Tic's radical ritual engaged to expel Epstein's spirit from the home/boarding house begins as a triangle – Leti, Tic, the Priestess – but not yet a circle. They chant in creole to Oyá, the Órísá whose domain is the cemetery. In the Yorùbá cosmology, Oyá is called upon to ensure right transition of the dead to the ancestral realm.

It's the bass for me.

"Tear Your Kingdom Down,"[10] featured during the radical ritual, was Shirley Caesar's 2011 arrangement of the spiritual, "Satan Your Kingdom Must Come Down," originally recorded in Chicago (site of the ritual and most of the series) by Blind Joe Taggart in 1931. Pastor Caesar's arrangement has become a Pentecostal anthem; it is a relentless march, and its sound creates an emotional charge by way of harmonies, moans, hums, and a downbeat stamp. Caesar calls, she ministers the entire track. Every line carries a tone that might have been born before her. Shortly after making their way to the basement, when the chanting in the ritual begins, the Priestess's body is taken by Epstein who tosses her across the room, stilling her to the floor. Epstein invisibly leaps from the Priestess's body to Tic. In the same moment, Pastor Caesar's voice, the choral hum, the stamp create a new call and the radical ritual shifts. Epstein's victims are invoked to not only become "the village" called to evict him, but to release themselves from unrested undead of the home/earthly plane to transition to the ancestral realm.

Three gestures of transformation happen: Tic/Epstein stamps to the middle of the room as he is encircled; the undead eight, the new village, metamorphose through a gifting back of their unmutated/unsliced/unimpaled bodies; Leti evolves as the appointed facilitator who ensures the radical ritual completes. Within the circle is a striking choreography. Tic's stomping and head shake, the eight's slow rise and peeling away of their injuries; it is a becoming and a leaving at the same time.

It ends. Spent in Holy Ghost and gore.

The employ of African Indigenous spirituality catalyzes and undergirds *Lovecraft Country.* And while Lovecraft does the important creative work of entering our ancestral lineages in futurist imaginings and projections, the remixing remixes out the portal openers and bearers of our spiritual technologies. Yearning for a Black queer radical in *Lovecraft* sits alongside a knowing that our Black futurities must include, because they are opened, dreamed and imbedded in the embodied of, Black queer and transgender people.

So go ahead, Lei: fly.

Yes, we are not (all) dead (although the murders of Black transwomen is a growing epidemic); we are not (all) in prison (although there we are made to suffer additional cruelties), yet, erasures treat us as not real either.

breathe

There is a linear understanding of the universe's expansion wherein after the big bang there was no time, and nothing existed (Cleggs 92–93)
… this is the big bang model based on Einstein's theory of relativity.

There is also a cyclical understanding of the universe that posits the universe underwent a series of contractions and expansions wherein time always existed and there was no singular "before."
…this is called a cyclic cosmology (Alexander 208) or what Dr. Stephon Alexander calls a "rhythmic universe."

In a cyclic cosmology we, at this time, are simply and complexly that: in this time. A part of a process of rhythmic shifts that will again and again embrace a next. It is a testimony to presencing.

A riff on Eckhart Tolle – infinite time has been broken down into religious and spiritual understandings. Religious frameworks articulate infinite time, language within a linear, vertical orientation. A spiritual or cosmic understanding interjects that time is an always, but that time is not forever. Not the same time anyway.

Telescopes are time portals, much like the practice of engaging with the cosmos spiritually or as a researcher. Cleggs offers, "as light travels at a finite speed (around 300,000 kilometers or 186,000 miles a second), the further away an object is, the further back in time we see it … In principle, with a good enough telescope, the furthest we can look back is around 13.5 billion years in time to where the universe became transparent when atoms formed. Before then, matter was electronically charged and soaked up any passing light."

Dark matter and dark energy, like all cosmic phenomena and understandings, are researched in the evidence of their pasts. What is unique to me about the way dark matter and dark energy are languaged: the word "dark" is invoked in science, to denote death, an annoyance, a "glitch in the matrix" or a rule break in astrophysics law. Something that is strange and unknown.

It is not just about the relationships between light and dark, interactions with light, but an aversion to darkness having its own logic. And at 96% it is the logic. Light, and all matter that can be directly seen, are actually the aberrations, what is directly observeable, articulated as "normal matter" is not, not in the least, certainly not in the most. The "most" of our universe is indirectly observeable, present only to us in its before, yet the pursuit of its understanding still centralizes what is by far the exception.

Unalive

"Unalived" is a phrase developed by social media content creators on TikTok, used to avoid violating community guidelines, infractions that are overwhelmingly and disproportionately deployed at Black creators. It is also, interestingly, an Africanist term.

"Unalived" is most often used as a verb, where to "unalive" someone means to murder them. I'm interested in the use of "unalive" as a noun. What is evoked when we think of someone as "unalive," not as in the "undead" Hollywood proposal of a carnivorous, evil, once human zombie dragging their feet across the land in search of warm, human blood. This portrayal of the "undead" is a literal demonization of complicated indigenous concepts of human and spiritual transition. An "undead" asserts that these between-states are horrific and dangerous for the living and the not yet dead.

Conversely, the "unalive" is a way of acknowledging both the physical or earthly transition of a life and an uplift of a spiritual presence and possibility. To be "unalived" is to be killed, but to be "unalive," like unarrival, is a state of the perpetual unknown, a presence that, like energy, cannot be killed.

There are concepts in astrophysics that rely on a collective consciousness where blackness and the dark are either simple menaces or are harbingers of death. For instance, a black dwarf is a theoretical stellar remnant that hypothesizes the final resting state of a dying star. It is a process that takes several billion years. "Black" because the white dwarf which is in the process of its death still emits some light, to a continually diminished degree because it longer undergoes nuclear fusion to give it energy or heat. It is believed that at some point the star will cool to the point of no longer emitting significant amounts of light or heat, thus transitioning. It becomes "black" by dying. And to be alive here means to light. Here, where its heat and light emissions levels are insignificant, death of a white dwarf is called black. An "unalived" star is a black one.

There are differences. Such as in the supernova, a star that is unalive and has transitioned to something with such light and directly observeable newness it is acknowledged as a new being altogether and not simply a dead star. Its death is a necessary liminality, to bring forth its new form. The supernova is a whole and individual entity.

Trans-embodiedness & Many Deaths

Blackness is so often seen in an unending past. The proliferation of Black death in inboxes, on timelines, and dominating news reports are circulations of antiblack erasure fantasy. This context of death and dying complicates for me the invocation of a "dead" anything in relationship to my trans identity. I am asking myself these days, "What of my identity is unalive?" or "antebecoming"?

Antebecoming is the always possibility of the/a next. I think of it as refusing to become: a method wherein blackness and Black people can, and do, reject permanence in contexts where our deaths are expected to be numerous, frequent, violent, and premature, or to be the example of what death, itself, looks like. To refuse to become, is to embody a cosmic circularity, to reject the stasis of white supremacy and its insistence upon Black people and blackness as temporal anecdotes.

So I am present to pauses.
Or agains.

The linear page betrays the transdirectionality of this thought I am in between space and ocean bottom Not quite flying Nor wholly suspended Vaporous or a spiral come nothing come an object before form This wants to be in multiple dimensions certainly not two However we linger in the ineptitude of a flat surface to
communicate ideas that will not sit still I kept feeling that my
experiments in in the dark were practices in astral travel and spiritual conjure
Something beyond the body was occurring as I was led to let the dark be the logic
and the lens I was attempting to understand its messaging the pulses of its theology
in the
material earth realm the quantum unreacheable the invisibility The dark kept pulling me into a familiar strange The presences were completely real and undeniable ancient otherly sensical and grand Cosmic real and not falsifiable thus not "scientific" however factual Seduced I searched for the just underneath above Like the dark up is a spectrum | | | | This will go between but it is not in contrast It is like the shadow of the Earth existing in relation and partnership and nothing like it Linked and distant

dripping in constellations
darkness/coded/invisible
striations/vibratory constants in
black/plenty obsidian/mural between
the outline/a fast memory of
flesh/neither facsimile nor projection

It is said that "anything relating Ifá to star gazing was developed in the Diaspora" (Abimbola) This does not diminish the potentialities in recognizing the ways in which the cultural practices metaphysical beliefs and mythologies in Ifá do correspond with astrophysics specifically and cosmic knowing more generally It strengthens in my opinion the veracity and resonances of Ifá's knowledges to allow for us to continue to reflect on the ways that the odu theologies or liturgy may have
application on planes beyond those initially conceived Invoking the +1 and in concert with my ori i trust that as a child of the Diaspora Órísá devotee listener and seer that my knowings and ruminations on these cosmic applications are not somehow untrue or impossible I exist within and was ancestrally invited through the +1 | | | |

Linked and distant: Standing 41 feet in the air on a catwalk outside of an 100-inch astronomical dome at mt wilson observatory at sunset You can feel the sacred Oak tree tops crows the splendid of mountain height and curvature making small of us i inhaled i exhaled at the quieting majesty I looked up at the dark to come as Dr. Tim Thompson pointed across the sky "Do you see that" "It's called the shadow of the Earth" This dark blue stretch seeming to float as it spread always opposite the rising or setting sun The shadow of the Earth makes an appearance as the sky changes The shadow ascends as and swallows the light then opens its mouth as it descends and shares the sky with day

"The law of the development of the universe is expressed through nature itself. Everything is first birthed out of darkness and this darkness is called the "womb of existence." This womb can be described as the black hole, the heavens the sum total of noumenal and phenomenal worlds, primordial waters of space, etc. Within this primordial womb, this oneness, lay infinite possibilities for expression.

"That womb is expressed as Olodumare in Yoruba, Mawu in Fon, Chineke in Igbo, Nut in ancient Kemet, Mumbi in Kikuyu, and Ataa-Naa Nyomo in GaDangme. This womb then gave birth to twins male and female or strong and yielding energy and these strong and yielding energies become the polarities expressed in the world as complementary opposites. Neither good or bad, better or worse, but natural expressions of energy within all things … it is important to keep in mind that this is simply a description of energy and is not to imply strict application to men and women. To do so will severely limit your understanding and application of the principles. Each are within us and in everything." (Awo Fategbe Fatunmbi Fasola, *The Holy Odu*)

There is hope in these lines through a transgender interpretation of gender and embodied experience. While, seemingly, stating "women" and "men" and "each" highlights or strictly demarcates gender in a particular way, the fact that we are encouraged to receive the naming of woman and man here, as energy and not gender, encourages me to think further about the spaces where these energies meet and the fact that given how each of us is so uniquely an expression of these energies, and more, and if it is the mix of matter that makes us who we are, then even the assertion of a singular or polar is nonsensical. It is the combination that creates. The law of the universe teaches over and over that change is all that one can expect.

In the cosmic womb of existence resides an indigenous source that understands the dark as a site of and generator of infinite imaginaries. Creation myths are made in the dark. In the context of the womb of existence where the energies, strong and yielding, complementary and different, precise but unfixed, are necessary to co-create *everything* that can materialize in the visible realm (*aiye*), which exists alongside the invisible world (orun). This cosmology articulates the possibilities beyond, yet that include dualities. African Indigeneity offers an understanding that these dualities are a starting place that give way to multiples.

In Yorùbá cosmology the cosmic womb gives birth to twins, *Eji Obge* and *Oyeku*. *Eji Ogbe* is understood as representing electromagnetism – "expansive light energy," referred to as the father, and as mover of "atoms, molecules, particles of creation." *Oyeku*, the mother, represents gravity or "contractive dark energy," pulling elements together "to create form like stars, planets" (Fasola 28). Again, these are not applied along fixed gendered lines, they are the indications of energy sources, not to be mistaken for overt dictations of gendered embodiment. What I am drawn to in this duality, is certainly the ways that the dark is connected as a Divine mother, but also the invocation of the dark as contracting, as gravity. It is a magical condensing of dark energy and dark matter together.

Dark energy "is responsible for the rapid acceleration of the universe's expansion" (Panek 168), and dark matter prevents the universe's implosion given that "matter attracts matter through gravity." This combination in Yorùbá, the framing of *Oyeku* as gravity *and* as an energy, presences what is

an emblematic simultaneity in Ifá and in other African Indigenous practices, and manifestations expressed throughout the Diaspora. As gravity, the dark is a womb capable of conjuring and materializing all things, and as energy it ensures the expansion of the universe. Inside the cosmic womb, one dark is the birthing of another dark. And others. And another. And.

This information is a kind of portal itself, is its own cosmic womb or even a cosmic map. The dark shows up in these old ways (including an understanding of the universe as an old way) and affirms for me that my research in dark matter and dark energy, all my dark dives and embodied practices, are extensions of Spiritual work. And while the lexicons and assumed applications may be distinct respectively, they are also offering possibilities between them. They, when read together, are a +1.

Black premature death suffocating us to leaving by way of anti-trans hate state sanctioned violences inequitable health care environmental racism predatory carceral structures asking for help teaching in universities internalization of overwork as a state of being houselessness mental health crisis jogging looking too male protesting wearing a hoodie living living living living breathing dreaming refusing the vitriol marches marathons of dying across necks while the bleeding of young black and trans ancestors line the walls of holy places the dark is not to blame for this mess

When I initially recognized that I must construct a physical environment to support the conduction of creative, spiritual, and metaphysical interweavings, it emerged after trying to make *Transtraterrestrial* in environments that couldn't possibly hold it. My first attempt was to "darken the institution"; I hung fabric, covered windows, turned off lights, taped everything that blinked. The white/ness of the spaces would not permit itself to be insignificant, despite being wholly unnecessary to the room. It was a vapid asseveration. Tiring. Distracting. After an attempt across the world and time zones across the united states to locate an approach to darkening or blackening that was liberatory and

aesthetically aligned, I learned that darkening the institution was extractive, depleting, and ultimately not my labor to do. I didn't want to make the work make sense in an environment constructed to decenter or outright reject what it takes to hear or abundantly receive its logics. Unarrival as a practice is in partnership with the dark, with invisibilities and morphologies. The dark, as the center, led everything, all the decisions. Invisibilities, the ability to be notice and be in one's physical world without relying on ocular sight to experience full embodiedness or presence. Unarrival itself a Black queer and trans shapeshifting practice. The morphology inherent in Unarrival practices allows, by millimeter and by lightyear, the escape of capture. By whispered prayer and guiding apparition, we make and remake, undo, and never land at a singularity. It is a sacred corporeality to be Black and unarrived.

I want to taste my life with my entire tongue

It was not going to be enough to try and inevitably fail to "transform" the politics and practices of the white box (or white theater or team or institution). The dark black necessary enough to practice unarrival and unconcealment could not be achieved by draping dense fabrics or taping over windows and exit signs. The theater spaces, as they were conceived, would simply not hold the blackness. Something had to be created from within the Unarrival universe. Beginning at architecture was too human. Too on the ground. I longed for another possibility that would allow me to find myself inside something so grand that it would be imperceptible. A space itself. So old, so first, so before, so beyond, that my body – not embodiedness – could be irrelevant. I could be, we could be, enormous inside that. Like my transness feels: so much bigger than my physicality, however beautiful the lines and melanin. To consider that my transness is inside that portal where blackness is at its wildest expression a liberating truth I choose to live into.

I imagine, on nights where the moon provides just enough softness for venus, that the stars i witness, dead and bright, catalyze their galactic resonances inside me.

We just out here being kindred.

Transtraterrestrial introduced the space | ship, a cosmic transportation devics of the dark to the dark. The work was originally titled *The Unarrival Experiements – Unconcealment Ceremonies*, and almost immediately demanded I vision bigger. The experiments in darkened spaces were deeply instructive, but they would not suffice. I needed *the* dark. I needed the dark where my own internalizations of the meanings of my body or racialized or gendered interpretations could, by creating conditions where the flesh could not be seen, but not disappeared, be felt, be immeasureable, and even more of itself. Its presence needed to be instantaneous, profound. I needed a space that could transport us beyond this plane, and together. I needed a spaceship. My own cosmic womb of creation.

Locating the space|ship became an epic process. I started with a geodesic dome shape in mind that I pursued for about two years, but after my first 3-week residency at the Experiment Media and Performing Arts Center (EMPAC) and several designs and drawings having failed to fully inspire or feel right, it became clear that I needed to continue to look inward to my own knowings and to, with Spirit, conjure forth a vessel. I asked "what can be an egbe itself, while also being a transportation vessel to one?" I went into VR and engaged in my movement conjure practice that I had been deeply in for at least as long as the dome had been conceived. From within that meditative movement session in the dark, I found it.

The space|ship, even as the very advanced prototype that was created for my prequel premiere at EMPAC was a powerful example for me, for the rest of my life, to maintain a commitment to protect, and insist, unrelentingly on vision.

•

To not know is not the same as not able.

•

In the ways that space and spirituality reframe darkness, these articulations of beginnings as dark and multiplicitous, I find the +1 inside myself. In my art, in *The Unarrival Experiments* constellation specifically, I am learning all the time how to listen to a wisdom that comes forth from unknowing. As artists, we are constantly creating universes that didn't exist and fighting, stretching, as we are transformed from their inceptions. The dark births from which I continue to ache along compel me to trust what I cannot see. Eyes open. Seeing nothing but
the black looking black at me.

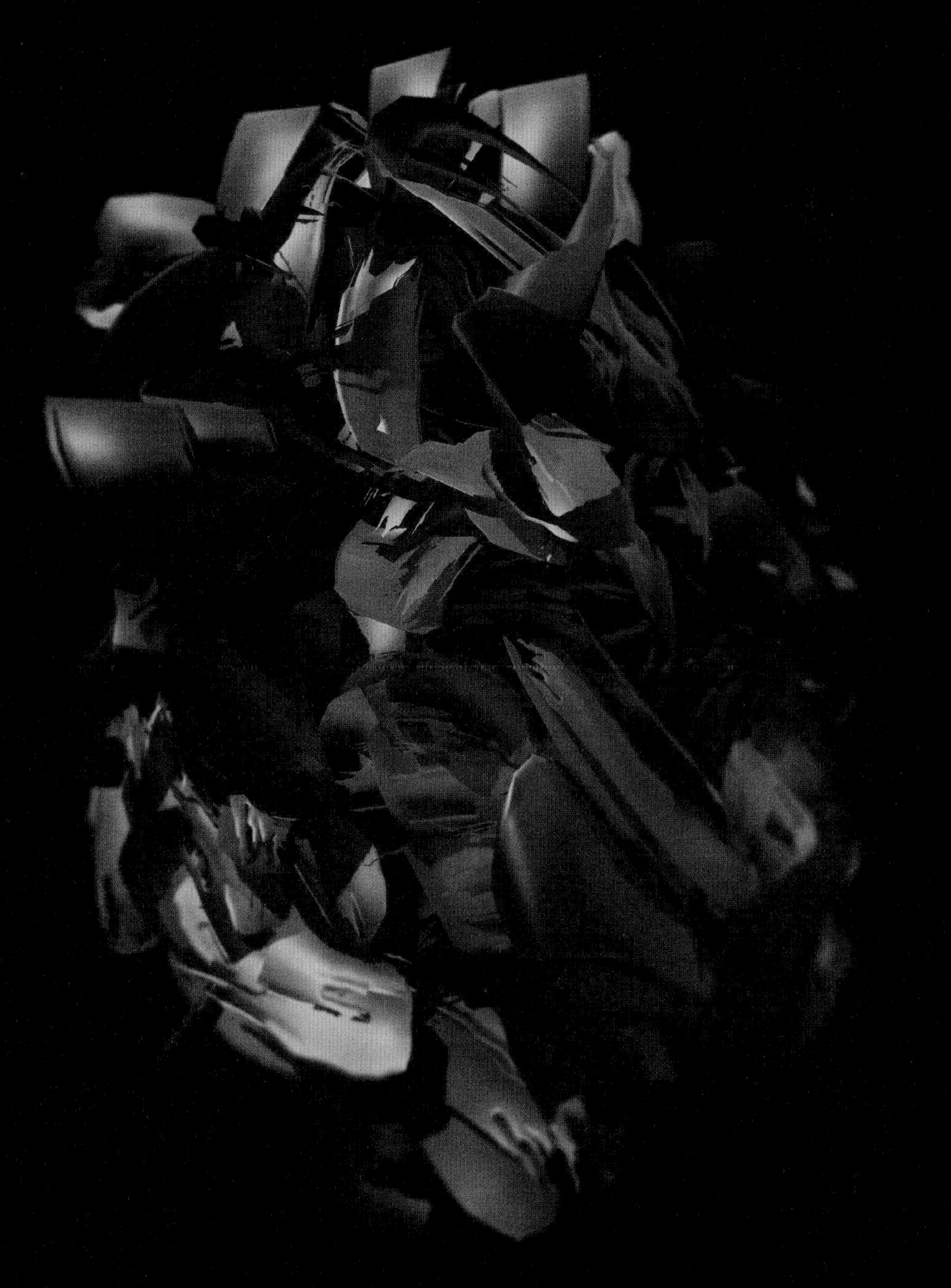

Of the cosmic womb
Beginning
To be birthed by
ancient
By time itself
To be stardust\we are
pieces of the galaxy
Even the motherless,
undermothered
Of us
Children sweetly
tended to by the stars
inside us
In that case I look in

Here
Move a cosmic body
Art a cosmic wisdom
Practice a cosmic
spirituality
Live inside a cosmic
joy
Stretch a cosmic
plurality

Dear, Monsters,
Dear, Witnesses,
Dear, Children I may never have,
Dear, Generations,
Dear, the Consequences of my living,
Dear, All my hungry days,
Dear the Body that carried me,
Dear, the Body I left,
Dear, the Being I became and alien that became me,
Dear, Foolishness,
Dear, Grief that chokes poetry I will not write,
Dear, the Waters,
Dear, Sorrows stitched in,
Dear, Pebbles in my shoe,
Dear, Courage,
Dear, Delight,
Dear, Forgotten,
Dear, Crooked letters,
Dear, Trap houses and birthdays,
Dear, Surprises painted as death,
Dear, Songbirds,
Dear, Thirst,
Dear, Long drives in unfamiliar longitude and latitudes,
Dear, Moving at the speed of soft,
Dear, Apologies,
Dear, Generations,
Dear, My mother's house,
Dear, Free tongues,
Dear, Crossed legs and herbal tea,
Dear, Good pussy,
Dear, Great pussy,
Dear, Falls and buoyant rises,
Dear, a Torniquet of harms,
Dear, Time trickled 'cross you,
Dear, Catastrophes,
Dear, I love you when it is the only thing the ancestors
will allow, which is always,
Dear, Silence,
Dear, Those who nap,
Dear, Playing in the dark,
Dear, for once.

Dear, Monsters,
Dear, Witnesses,
Dear, Children I may never have,
Dear, Generations,
Dear, the Consequences of my living,
Dear, All my hungry days,
Dear the Body that carried me,
Dear, the Body I left,
Dear, the Being I became and alien that became me,
Dear, Foolishness,
Dear, Grief that chokes poetry I will not write,
Dear, the Waters,
Dear, Sorrows stitched in,
Dear, Pebbles in my shoe,
Dear, Courage,
Dear, Delight,
Dear, Forgotten,
Dear, Crooked letters,
Dear, Trap houses and birthdays,
Dear, Surprises painted as death,
Dear, Songbirds,
Dear, Thirst,
Dear, Long drives in unfamiliar longitude and latitudes,
Dear, Moving at the speed of soft,
Dear, Apologies,
Dear, Generations,
Dear, My mother's house,
Dear, Free tongues,
Dear, Crossed legs and herbal tea,
Dear, Good pussy,
Dear, Great pussy,
Dear, Falls and buoyant rises,
Dear, a Torniquet of harms,
Dear, Time trickled 'cross you,
Dear, Catastrophes,
Dear, I love you when it is the only thing the ancestors
will allow, which is always,
Dear, Silence,
Dear, Those who nap,
Dear, Playing in the dark,
Dear, for once.

NOTES

“Super Fluid / Super Black: Translations and Teachings in Transembodied Metaphysics”

1 In this section I looked to sources that were accessible and readily available online in order to evaluate the developing ways that histories of Diaspora are disseminated and collected in the cyber global sphere.

2 Edwidge Danticat, “The Long Legacy of Occupation in Haiti.” *The New Yorker*, July 28, 2015. Accessed February 2, 2020, www.newyorker.com/news/news-desk/haiti-us-occupation-hundred-year-anniversary/; and “U.S. Invasion and Occupation of Haiti, 191534.” Office of the Historian, Foreign Service Institute, https://history.state.gov/milestones/1914-1920/haiti. https://history.state.gov/milestones/1914-1920/haiti.

3 “Carnegie Corporation Oral History Project.” Columbia University Libraries of Oral History Research Office, www.columbia.edu/cu/lweb/digital/collections/oral_hist/carnegie/special-features/.

4 “How Sweet the Sound: Gospel Music in Los Angeles.” Exhibition, California African American Museum, February 8–August 26, 2018.

5 It should be noted that, as the passage suggests, this number is given with as few as 24 and as many as 28. I elected to quote the higher number given the understanding that these crimes went largely undocumented. See Francis Jacobs, “Chilling Maps of Lynchings in 1930s America.” April 6, 2018, https://bigthink.com/strange-maps/chilling-maps-of-lynchings-in-1930s-america.

6 From the unpublished manuscript of *The Unarrival Experiments*.

7 Jacob Williamson-Rea, “Physicist theorizes that dark matter is superfluid,” in *Penn Today*, September 17, 2018, https://penntoday.upenn.edu/news/physicist-theorizes-dark-matter-superfluid; and Michael Irving, “Dark matter and dark energy may really be one ‘dark fluid’ with negative mass,” in *New Atlas*, December 6, 2018, https://newatlas.com/dark-fluid-theory-matter-energy/57540.

8 “TMM Update Trans Day of Remembrance 2019,” Trans Respect Versus Transphobia Worldwide. November 11, 2019, https://transrespect.org/en/tmm-update-trans-day-of-remembrance-2019/.

9 SA Smythe, “Can I Get a Witness? Black Feminism, Trans Embodiment, and Thriving Past the Fault Lines of Care.” Unpublished article, 2020. Used with permission of the author.

“‘You are not in prison,’ ‘You are not real’: Transmutation, Time, and the Yearning for a Black Queer Radical in *Lovecraft Country*”

1 Sobonfu E. Somé, *The Spirit of Intimacy: Ancient Teaching in the Ways of Relationships* (New York: William Morrow, 2000), 133–36.

2 Malidoma Somé, *The Healing Wisdom of Africa: Finding Life Purpose Through Nature, Ritual, and Community* (New York: Tarcher, 1999), 149.

3 Malidoma Somé, “Grief, Ritual, Sacrifice.” Video, www.youtube.com/watch?v=Y7I97ebNn0I/.

4 Che Gossett, "In Blackness and the Trouble of Trans Visibility," in *Trap Door: Trans Cultural Production and the Politics of Visibility*, eds. Reina Gossett, Eric A. Stanley, and Johanna Burton (Cambridge, MA: MIT Press, 2017), 185.

5 Gossett, 183.

6 Gossett, 184.

7 Allen Drexell, "Gay Life in 1950's Bronzeville: The Story of Jacques Cristion," https://outhistory.org/exhibits/show/queer-bronzeville/part-2/jacques-cristion; and Tristan Cabello, "Queer Bronzeville," https://outhistory.org/exhibits/show/queer-bronzeville/part-2/drag-balls/.

8 *National Geographic*, www.nationalgeographic.com/animals/invertebrates/facts/locusts; and "About Locusts," Australian Government Department of Agriculture, Water, and the Environment, www.agriculture.gov.au/pests-diseases-weeds/locusts/about/about_locusts#what-is-the-difference-between-a-locust-and-a- grasshopper/.

9 Malidoma Somé, "Grief, Ritual, Sacrifice."

10 Shirley Caesar, *Platinum Gospel*, featuring Institutional Radio Choir. Sonorous Records, 2011.

Counterproposals Image Archive

Transtraterrestrial, 2023 – Prequel and Premiere | pg. 56 |
Experimental Media and Performing Arts Center (EMPAC)
Photo Credit: Michael Valiquette, Courtesy of EMPAC

A Black Technologic: Considering Liberatory Imaginaries in Emerging Technologies, 2022 – EMPAC | pg. 84–92 |
The images on pages 84–92 are documentation/performance stills from a talk given at the Experimental Media and Performing Arts Center, where I presented my work with Virtual Reality (VR) as it relates to the creation of the then-upcoming EMPAC production and performance of *Transtraterrestrial*. As an extension of the design and research process, the talk proposed new futures for VR with questions that begged to remain unanswered.
Photo Credit: Alvis Mosely, Courtesy of EMPAC

Watermill Arts Center Residency, 2019 | pg. 93 |
Photo Credit: Maria Baranova-Suzuki

VR Rendering of space|ship, 2023 | pg. 121 |
Photo Credit: Artist